CHILDREN and grieving

JANET GOODALL

First published 1995

Revised edition 1999

Scripture Union, 207-209 Queensway,
Bletchley, Milton Keynes MK2 2EB, England

ISBN 0 86201 866 8

British Library Cataloguing–in–Publication Data.
A catalogue record for this book is available from the British Library.

Phototypeset by Intype, London.
Printed and bound in Great Britain by Cox and Wyman Ltd, Reading.

Contents

Thankyous

The first thanks must go to the families who have taught me so much. Many of them share their stories now with the hope that they will help somebody else.

For arousing my interest in how children think I must thank Caroline Lister, educational psychologist, and my dear sister-in-law, Joan Goodall, one-time lecturer at Froebel College. I began to apply their insights to dying children after receiving a challenge from Jennifer Chapman, who was a junior doctor on our paediatric team at the North Staffordshire Hospital Centre, Stoke-on-Trent. Later work inspired her to see and to report back the urgent need for paediatric terminal care. I remain grateful, both to her and to other senior medical and nursing colleagues, who then joined us in thinking through how best to help dying and bereft children.

We learned a lot from their parents. David and Jean Hudson, then Roland and Jenny Wakefield, changed our views on dying babies; Marilyn and Graham Cotton, Sarah and Dick Bowen and, later, Phil Carlson gave more insights about older children. Gwen Belsire gives her lovely account of Christopher in chapter 3.

Bishop Keith Sutton of Lichfield graciously spared precious time to comment on chapter 11. Sarah and Andrew have allowed me to quote from their school essays and Emma from her memories of a beloved brother's death. Jenny Kimber of BBC Radio Stoke shared her award-winning interview with bereaved school children and their teachers. Laurie and Sheila Beard offered a hideaway and Ellen Dayson provided her flat as a peaceful haven in which to finish the manuscript. I am so grateful to all these good friends for their great help.

John Wyatt, a consultant paediatrician at University College Hospitals, London, also gave helpful advice on the structure and style of the book.

Elrose Hunter, a commissioning editor at Scripture Union, initially asked me to write on this subject. Her gentle insistence that we keep on trying to get it right, together with the support of many other praying friends, has brought the book to birth. Our shared prayer is for it to be an instrument of help and healing to all those who read it.

Finally, I thank God for being there in all the shadowed places and for sowing and growing the seed thoughts of which this is now the fruit. May it convey a sense of the Lord's goodness.

Preface

Whatever our age, grief comes to us in many forms, but the worst bereavement of all is to lose a loved one.

Everyone feels upset when someone dies, especially when little children are left behind yet, despite all the concern and sympathy, no-one may know quite what to say to the younger members of a bereaved family. This can end up with either nothing being said to them at all or the telling of an unconvincing story. I heard recently of the death of an old Scotswoman whose grandchildren were told that she was now looking down on them from a cave. It is good to be imaginative but bad to substitute fantasy for truth, however painful the truth may be.

We were all children once, but even professional advisers may have forgotten how to take a child's eye view of things. The first lesson may be to become like children ourselves and not to flinch from calling death by its name.

Christians, wanting to help children to come to terms with loss, may for a time be lost for words themselves. We can all be utterly perplexed when the burden of human suffering hits home, including hurt for children, and may even wonder where the God of love is now. It can be the children themselves who remind us how a living relationship with him is at the heart of faith. He walks the valleys with us.

Children vary. They have different levels of understanding, which relate not only to their age but also to experience. Tuning in to the right wavelength is vital if we are to help a grieving child. This is explained more fully on page 33.

We shall be looking at and learning from two groups of children: those whose loved ones die and those who are themselves dying. The main focus will be on helping each child's personal needs. The care of the dying child's physical state, including details of drug therapy, will not be dealt with here. Some of the professional references supplied will give more of that kind of information.

When I have been able to trace parents for permission, and that is so for most of them, their stories use the real names of the children in gratitude for lessons learned from them. Some budded without blossoming, but still bear fruit.

1

How can we tell the children?

Someone special is about to die or has suddenly died. The adults in a family understand all too well what is going on, but what about the children? How should bad news be broken to them? Ought they to be told at all? Worst of all are the awful tidings which, at a stroke, reduce life expectancy for the children themselves. Perhaps it is true that ignorance is bliss and they would be happier not to know.

Ignorance is not bliss

A few years ago I was discussing this kind of dilemma with a group of young doctors. We all listened in stunned silence as one of them quietly told us how, at the age of eleven, her mother had sent her off to a party. When she came back her father was not there, but the atmosphere was so strange that she did not dare ask where he was. It was six years later, when she was seventeen years old, that her mother told her that he had died whilst she was out and his body had been removed. It was perhaps significant that he had been a doctor and that she was now training to be a children's doctor, wanting to help other hurting children.

A friend of mine went through a similar experience when she was only six years old. She came home from school to find no Daddy, but everyone making a great fuss of her little sister. Later she learned that her father had unexpectedly died of a heart attack, with the younger daughter on his bed at the time. The shock had caused this child to lose all power in her legs, adding great anxiety to the already distraught mother's own shock and grief. None of this was explained to the older child at the time, who suddenly found her homecoming had landed her into the middle of something she could not understand. She felt left out in the cold.

Worse still, the change in family circumstances which followed the father's death meant that her mother needed to go out to work. The bewildered six year old then had to come home to an empty house, terrified that just as her father had suddenly disappeared, so her mother might not reappear either. Unexplained, these events left emotional scars which lasted for years, though she also grew up to be very sensitive to the needs of others who needed support.

Stories like these challenge the idea that it is best not to say anything to a child about a death in the family. Yet our television screens also show us the faces of children who have just been told about, or have even witnessed, the violent death of a loved one and we dread causing similar desolation to our own bereft children. How can we even start to tell them something so awful? As we have seen, children can be more hurt by not being told the truth than by being sensitively included in the reality of the sadness. It can be so helpful for everyone to be grieving together openly.

Children pick up atmosphere

Children are like barometers of feeling, reflecting changes in the family atmosphere. They know when something is wrong, but to be left out of the secret, particularly when very young, can make them feel that they themselves have done something unspeakably awful. Children are very familiar with being at the heart of an upset and having a good cry. An explanation, properly given, can actually bring a degree of relief that the trouble has been none of their doing, even though at the same time the news is of something very upsetting.

Heaven is where the heart is

Christian parents might take a different view, telling their children that the family member who has disappeared has been taken by Jesus and is now in heaven. After this kind of information, one four year old girl refused to go to Sunday School any more. She wanted nothing further to do with someone who took grannies away like that to a destination nobody seemed able to explain properly. Yet another child of the same age, having been told that her auntie had gone to be with Jesus, commented a few days later, 'She must be having such a great time with him.' To think of a loved one still sharing in an already treasured relationship could be more comforting than to try to imagine an unknown place.

Children are not mini-adults

The first thing for us to remember as adults is that children are not just pocket editions of ourselves. We must also avoid thinking that, just because we call them all 'children', they will look at things in the same way as each other. A toddler's view of the world will differ from a seven year old's just as a seven year old's so clearly differs from a teenager's.

Different temperaments also mean that what sends one child into a temper tantrum may make another become very subdued and quiet. Each child is an individual, whose character traits are usually obvious fairly early on to those who care for them.

There are therefore no set rules about discussing difficult subjects with children. Their questions can often strike adults as being unexpected and awkward, although each child clearly thinks that these are the obvious things to ask. In order to help us to see behind the question to the confusion which has sometimes prompted it, we do need a few guidelines about the probable viewpoint of a child in any particular age group.

We will be looking for these guidelines in chapter 2, but we need first to take a quick look at ourselves. Such guidelines will be of little use if we are not of a mind to use them. As we have learned, perhaps from experience, grief can knock people sideways. The first response to bad news or to bereavement itself can be to feel so shocked or so empty that thinking about others at all is a huge effort.

Adult responses to grief

There are already many books written about bereavement in general, but you have picked up this particular one because you want to know more about the grief of children. Yet it is relevant to touch first on how adults react both to hearing bad news and then being bereaved by a death, because the very first reaction in either case can be one of *denial*. Due to the very numbness which grief so often brings, or by the natural desire to blot out what is happening, the needs of children can be temporarily overlooked or even totally neglected.

Some Christians show another form of denial by believing that we should take everything from the hand of God without complaint. Expressions of grief are regarded as murmurings against him and must therefore be sternly put aside. It is as well to remember how the shortest verse in the Bible tells us that 'Jesus wept.' (John 11:35) He, too, shared in the grief which followed a dear friend's death.

Searching is possibly another form of denial, but also a natural response to the experience of loss. It is irrational and hard to control, but not unusual. In life we look for a cure for our loved ones and after their death long to see them again, sometimes even mistaking someone in the street for one who has gone. Searching and *pining* often take turns as predominant emotions.

Anger may flare up and surprise a previously peaceable person, who may say or do things entirely out of character. This can add to *guilt*, which is often there already, or turn it to *blame*. The bringer of bad news, or one who is thought to have hastened the death, will often be blamed for it. It is not unusual for this to be a doctor, but bereft and angry people can say wounding words which put the blame on to someone else, even within the family.

Bargaining can be detected in a remark such as, 'If only we can still have her here for Christmas,' when a family faces an inevitable death. Alternatively, 'We could accept it if only we knew how the accident happened,' may be said after a sudden loss. This state of mind can then descend into *depression* as it is realised that these hopes are not going to be met.

It can take much longer than most people realise before the whirlpool of mixed emotions becomes calmer and there is a gentle *coming-to-terms* with loss. It is hard to generalise, but to lose a member of the immediate family is a major loss for most people and it can be even a year or more before each day ceases to bring new pangs. To speak of 'being over it' or 'accepting it' is something which most deeply grieving people will find it hard to do, even after a number of years.

Grief has to be faced

There may be a spiritual sense in which it is accepted that God has allowed the death to happen. There can be joy for the one who has gone, but still deep sorrow may remain for those left behind. Emotions must be experienced, acknowledged and allowed to recover before, deep down, mind and heart can reach a measure of ease again.

How long the hurt takes to heal and how well it does so after a death can depend on whether this was sudden or expected, easy or painful and how close the lost relationship was. It will also be affected by the personality of the bereaved person and how previous losses have been dealt with. To try to lock away feelings behind a brave face may only store up trouble for the future.

Grief can be turbulent and terrible and its consequences long-lasting. Even when it might have been expected that the end of a long illness would come as a relief to everyone, sorrow can still descend with surprising force. Later, grief may resurface when there are other, even relatively minor, losses or on the anniversaries of a dear one's birth and death.

The process of healing is made easier by friends who understand that recovery takes a long time.

Meanwhile, God's own promises offer both comfort and hope. He has said that he will never leave us or forsake us, even when we go through deep waters.

The Lord Jesus, when facing his own death, encouraged his grieving disciples with the thought that he was going to prepare a place for them to be with him. His presence and his provision are still on offer today.

Children are affected by the grief of adults

It is not hard to see how a climate of continuing tension within a grieving family will be picked up but not properly understood by young children unless someone takes the time and trouble to explain it to them. That sensitive 'someone' may be a trusted family friend, minister, school teacher or other counsellor if parents, for example, are still too stunned to manage by themselves. The important thing is that the children's needs should not be denied.

Rather than listening to any more theory let us now hear from the parents of a five year old boy who had cancer. His parents learned important lessons as they cared for him and his sisters. Here is the first, introduced by their father:

'When the subject of telling the children was broached to me, I was quite horrified. I didn't think that this was the right way to go about it. Now I realise that it was. It would be so easy for a father to put his foot down and say, "No", but now I must say that I think it is important.'

His wife added: 'We both feel very strongly about this point. When I was a young child, I remember that an aunt died and I was told that she had gone to live with somebody else. It was later in life that I realised that she hadn't really, she had died. I was horrified that they could make up such tales. I was also helped by having lost a brother later on, when I was a young girl. I wanted our children to share with us because I was so grateful to my parents that this time they had shared everything.'

Whose death are we talking about?

A child will feel the loss of anyone who has been close, including a pet or a best friend, but the closest ties are likely to have been with immediate members of the family. To lose a parent in early life is probably one of the greatest possible griefs with the longest after-effects, unless the children's needs are recognised and help provided.

The loss of brothers and sisters is sad, not only because of the personal impact but because of the added sense of responsibility which may follow. Bereaved children can feel that they must somehow try to make up for the family's loss before they have had time to grieve properly themselves. It is also worth remembering, when a baby is born too soon to survive or is stillborn, that it will be easier for other children in the immediate family to understand what has happened if they are included when goodbyes are being said.

Grandparents and their grandchildren often share a very special relationship and for many children the loss of such a beloved person is their first experience of death. Other relationships need to be seen from the child's point of view. Favourite aunts and uncles, even of the adopted variety, can be close and special people in a child's eyes. It is not always recognised how close a child's cousins or school friends can be, or how devastating it may be to lose a pet.

Our greatest worry may be how to recognise and relieve the grief of children who face their own death.

Noticing a child's grief

My experience as a children's doctor has naturally been more to do with the deaths of children than of adults. Most of my examples are therefore about dying children and those bereaved by their deaths, though reactions are likely to be similar when other key figures die. It is sometimes easy for grown-ups to think that little children are not upset, as their grief does not usually show itself in the same ways as ours. However, not until adolescence will a child's grief so clearly follow the pattern of adult grief which we have been looking at, so we need to stay tuned.

When to get help for a grieving child

If a child has witnessed a violent death or has unexpectedly lost a parent, it would be wise to seek advice as soon as possible. If outside help is not available, it is vital that someone in the circle of family and friends realises and responds to the child's urgent need for personal support and understanding.

When there has been time for preparation and inclusion of the child after the death of a close relative, grief is still to be expected but usually follows a natural sequence over a period of weeks or months. We shall see later what this is likely to be at different ages. (See pages 54, 86, 110, 141, 159.) If acute grief is severe enough to cause serious concern, the local doctor or practice nurse would be the natural first port of call. A local counselling service for children is still a relative rarity, but will offer wise help when there is one available. There is a list of helpful agencies on pages 191–192.

An understanding ear will in the long run be more helpful than a lot of sedation, though occasionally a doctor may advise a short course of medication. If this is the case, it should not be thought of as a rather dubious remedy for a Christian to take. Like paracetamol for a headache, or a bandage for a sprained ankle, such treatment is a short term support to bring relief until natural healing gets underway. In the long term, though, the evidence is that children who are included in and supported through a bereavement fare better than others who have been kept in the dark.

Whether they are bereaved or dying, the way in which young children look at death will be governed by the ways in which they regard life, so the time has now come to get down to the guidelines.

Points for grieving adults to remember:

*Children are used to being upset and may blame themselves for causing trouble.

*Being kept out of family grief can be sadder than being included.

*In their own first reaction of denial in grief, adults can overlook a child's needs.

Helpful Bible passages:

Psalm 23

John 14:1–4

Philippians 4:6,7

Isaiah 43:1–3a

Further reading:

Mary Bending, *Caring for bereaved children* (Richmond, Cruse-Bereavement Care 1993).

Dora Black, 'Bereavement', in Ann Goldman (ed.) *Care of the dying child* (Oxford, Oxford University Press 1994) chapter 9.

Celia Hindmarch, *On the death of a child* (Oxford, Radcliffe Medical Press 1993).

Elaine Storkey, *Losing a child* (Illinois, Lion Publishing Corporation 1989).

2

How children think

Across the United Kingdom there are a number of clothes shops bearing the trade name, 'High and Mighty'. It is obvious at once that people will not go there to buy clothes for children. Most families take care to dress their young in styles and sizes suited to them. When going out for a meal, they may also prefer to go to a place offering a 'Kids' Special'. A society which is tuned in to children knows that their needs are different from those of the adult population.

Yet when it comes to giving information to children, we may either offer it in adult dimensions so that it does not fit their minds, or present it in an indigestible way. One alternative is to tell them nothing at all, thinking that they are too young to understand. However, a child too young to eat beefsteak could be given the meat minced up, or even as beef tea, not simply left to starve. To plead to the magistrates that, 'He was too little to eat our steak,' would not excuse criminal neglect. Yet how often are children told, 'You're too little to understand,' and so made to feel left out in the cold, unsatisfied.

Learning again how to think like a child

The only excuse there is for failing to feed children's minds properly is ignorance, not on their part, but on ours.

We need to know how to predigest information for any particular child and how to carry on discussion in a fitting way.

Guidelines, not tramlines

When we go shopping for children's clothes, the manufacturer's labels will often give an idea as to which age range they are designed for. This is only a *rough* estimate, though. Every mother knows how her '3 to 5 year old' suddenly needs to wear T-shirts in the '6 to 8 year old' category, or is still skinny enough to take a smaller size. This does not mean that the manufacturer's labels are misleading. They simply provide a useful guide for getting into the right area to find something likely to fit.

In just the same way, it is the sequence of the child's development which is important. This means that the chapter headings later on are not precisely tailor-made for a child in each of the age groups described. Like labels on off-the-peg clothes, they are there to guide towards something

approximately suitable but may overlap in either direction. Listening carefully to the child is like trying to find the right fit. We may often be surprised to find a maturity ahead of what we had expected, as well as the opposite. Some ideas could be applied to all ages, so it is worth looking through the book and matching these to individual needs.

How to begin

When trying to buy new clothes or to share new ideas with young children it is safer to start with something which we know will fit and then move on from there. To begin at the beginning, the smallest people of all, the babies, can give us a sure foundation (a sort of 'free size') which will suit anyone at all as we start the attempt to clothe ideas in ways suited to them.

Babies are born ready to love other people and they literally thrive best when loved in return. It is, then, in an atmosphere of caring attentiveness that all interaction will flourish best, from the cradle to the grave.

The early months

During the first day of life, a baby can show great *interest in other people*. (Early smiles are not due to wind any more than later ones are!) Interest grows steadily, but it is probably several months before infants realise that those who arrive in answer to their calls have lives of their own to lead.

Babies, as well as older children, can be *barometers of feeling*, picking up from the atmosphere around them both happiness and tension.

The concept of permanence develops during an infant's first year. It has arrived when the child understands that a person or object is still there, even when out of sight. We can check whether this idea has developed or not by hiding under a cover something with which the baby was playing. Even though the infant watched carefully all that we did, we will not usually see the cover pulled away and the object reclaimed before the first eight to ten months of life. Although the idea of the permanence of people possibly comes a few months earlier, until it comes, out of sight is thought to mean out of existence.

'*Me, here, now*', is the outlook of children for at least their first eighteen months. An adult who betrays this kind of outlook would be called egocentric, but young children cannot think in any other way, so should not be blamed for it. Although books on behaviour do refer to this 'me, here, now' phase as 'egocentric', I prefer to call it the 'me-centred' stage. Thinking first from one's own viewpoint is common to us all, but infants have no choice about it.

Eighteen months to about three years

What a lovely age to be! So many new and wonderful things are going on. To get up and go unaided, so making the adults speed after you; to say a few words, thus impressing everyone; to start building with blocks or matching up shapes must all be so exciting.

Matching is the basic skill being learned now. It will become more refined as the years go by, but will be in constant use from now on. The circle fitted into its slot on the shape board at one year old can in another year be crudely copied onto a piece of paper. Two circles drawn one above the other and suitably bewhiskered will soon be identified as 'Pussy'. It will be some years yet, though, for two small circles on top of each other to be recognised and copied as the figure eight and about twice as long again before a child could work out how to follow this pattern when roller-skating.

The use of *power* is now being learned and practised. 'No' is one of the earliest words to be used, having been so often heard! Now is the time when 'No' is put to great use in provoking all kinds of interesting gyrations amongst grown-ups. This is therefore known by the pundits as the stage of *negativism*. It must give the child a wonderful sense of being in control. Yet, if there are no secure limits, it can be terrifying to find things instead going quite out of control. For a child to feel safe, *limits are needed*.

To be taught where the limits lie is the major discipline of toddlerhood. To go back to basics, love is what matters most. Add to this the young child's skill in matching and we have a recipe for both teaching and learning, patiently and consistently, that some behaviour brings warmth and happiness whilst another kind brings the opposite. If too harsh, discipline brings fear and if too lax, wilfulness. Balance has to be worked for.

Real love is not sloppy but strong. Firm affection and affectionate firmness together will make a child feel secure. Learning to make other people happy can become an underlying rule of life, even without at first knowing why it is that some things please and others do not. In some families, approval can be harder to come by than disapproval, but both are needed for a child to achieve acceptable behaviour.

A basic error of the child's thinking now is that *things are just as they appear to be*. This can cause so much misunderstanding between adults and young children. From a two year old's standpoint, the tablecloth looks firm enough to hold on to for support. It is important for adults to remember this outlook when tempted to judge the child's behaviour only through their own eyes. It is catastrophic enough for the contents of the breakfast table to have arrived unexpectedly about a child's head without parental wrath descending on it as well.

Errors of judgment should not mean that the one who has erred is called naughty. Such a domestic disaster would be an opportunity to point out that tugging at the tablecloth is not a good thing to do. This may have to be said patiently and firmly, over and over again, before it is memorised. Only then can obedience be reasonably expected.

The range of about three to about seven years old

Matching and mismatching continue and *face-value judgment* persists. One way to check this is to take two tumblers of water, containing an equal volume in each, and to empty one into a taller, thinner container as the child watches. Throughout most of this age group (if the child can play the game at all) it will be assumed that there is more water where the level looks higher. This conclusion still comes as a slight shock to me, even after doing the test so often. Until they have gained more experience, children simply do not look at things as we do.

This can be a protection, in that the implications of something are not yet being worked out. It can also give rise to great bewilderment. This is a time when *imagination is very busy*, with facts and fancies often getting confused. The child can make huge efforts to work out why something seems to have changed when it has not really done so, or to connect two things which really have no connection with each other at all.

Let's see how this could happen. Imagine that you are three again and have such a bad cough that for the first time you need physiotherapy to your chest. Only this morning, you were corrected by your mother for holding your little sister over the arm of the settee and thumping her on the back, yet now this is exactly what a total stranger seems to be doing to you. Could this be some kind of punishment? Mummy never thumps, but she is standing by and not stopping it. To add to the mystery, they are both saying that this will make your cough better, but it is actually making you cough so hard that you want to be sick. It is all very odd.

A child at the 'Me, here, now' stage will accept as part of ordinary life some routine which is really extraordinary, but the introduction of something previously not experienced needs to be explained in easily digestible terms. The physiotherapist could have told your three year old self that the cough was due to some stuff, its proper name being 'mucus', which was tickling the inside of your throat. She was going to tap it out, rather like you tap out ketchup from a bottle, but it would look a lot different from the ketchup. When the mucus had all gone, the cough would go, too. With this explanation, the possibility of the little sister's part in the affair would probably not even have come to mind.

Matching how someone else may be *feeling* can be shown by little children, for example when trying to comfort someone who is crying. They use methods which they have experienced personally. It can still be *hard to make logical links* until the latter end of this age range. Imaginative fantasies, including invisible friends, are normal. Persistent 'me-centredness' also means *failure to observe being different from others*. This combination protects young children with chronic disease from grasping that their illness sets them apart from others. Truth may dawn at the same time as the ability comes to recognise the right answer in the water-in-the-tumbler test. To realise that, 'It must still be the same because it was the same to start with,' is also to see that, 'I can't be the same as others because they don't have my treatment.' For the first six or seven years of life, an average child would be protected from this sharp awareness, though an experienced or bright child would learn earlier.

Words can have inner meanings, or none. The word 'mucus' will mean little to a child until able to match the word to the substance. Yet it could still be repeated, learned and even used properly, long before its implications were understood. *Double meanings are grasped slowly,* so that it takes time to realise that the same word can have more than one meaning. Until this possibility is grasped, a child may have secret reservations, for example, about stroking the cat, if told that 'Granny died after a stroke.'

Starting school, even nursery school, is (after the initial shock of being born!) one of the biggest upheavals of childhood. Whether this turns out to be stressful or thrilling, it can bring a marked growth spurt in understanding as 'same' and 'not the same' are applied with a greater choice of options than ever before.

The range of about seven to about eleven years old

Skill in making deductions is growing, but *face value judgment still trails along* as well. This could be one of the most confusing ages to belong to, as the intertwining of these two ways of thought means that *arriving at wrong conclusions* is a very common experience.

At the start of this period, many children do not yet realise that their thoughts are private, or that other people may think differently. There is still *no real insight* into someone else's viewpoint unless skill in matching combines with personal past experience, although a naturally caring disposition will also help a child to identify with the problem. I was once telling the Bible story of Lazarus to a group of children. As Billy, aged five, heard how Lazarus had felt so poorly that he had stayed in bed and hadn't even wanted Martha's nice breakfast, his eyes lit up with understanding. 'He'd got the measles!' he said.

Greater scope for comparing one thing with another during the matching process also means that the child *starts to notice inequality and unfairness*. Applied to self as well as to anyone else, this may highlight disadvantages but it can also call forth a new *concern for others*. 'It's not fair' can be widely applied and is a familiar cry from this age group.

It is still helpful to work something out with a visual aid, though towards the end of this age range *working it out in the head* begins. Simple mental arithmetic, or the ability to describe a well-trodden route without a plan, become the latest new skills. Today's general increase in visual input, though, may delay the development of such mental elasticity. Computer skills are based on matching more than reasoning, which is why children are often so good at them.

It is still hard to have accurate images, such as of inside the body. Matching ideas would help, such as the lungs being likened to balloons which blow up as we breathe in. However, as we blow up real balloons by breathing out, trying to clarify the body's unseen activities may still be quite difficult.

Although puns and riddles, with their play on words, are now great fun, the inner meaning of *proverbs and parables* is still *not understood*, though their obvious outer meaning can be worked out logically, step by step. A ten year old knew that when Granny said, 'Too many cooks spoil the broth,' she wanted her out of the kitchen, but she could not interpret the inner meaning of the proverb or apply it to other activities.

The average child in this age range still has *no clear recognition of implications* and *no clear-sighted looking ahead*. Imagination can still be active, though, and can cause needless anxiety. I remember finding an eleven year old in his hospital bed, rigid with terror. His illness did not warrant this, but he eventually screwed up enough courage to ask, 'When am I going to have my operation?' All he knew about hospitals was that people go there to undergo surgery. Certain television programmes can fuel this kind of worry.

The range of about twelve years old into adolescence

This is when thinking, at last, *approaches adult thought* in method, though not in maturity. It has taken a long time. The ability to *reason in the abstract*, without visual aids, has now arrived, together with greater ability to perform *mental gymnastics*, running rings round others in debate and discussion. *Idealism* (as well as vegetarianism!) may swing into action.

This greater elasticity of thought means that the child has a clearer *awareness of implications and expectations*. Leaping to a conclusion is now more likely to land on the right answer. *Explanations can be followed logically* and a description or diagram can now be more readily applied to events going on inside the body. Most twelve year olds would demonstrate this expansion of mental outlook by correctly judging, by eye only, the equal volumes of water in containers of different shapes, even without first having witnessed the exercise which changed their appearance. *Judgment has become internalised*, so the child now arrives at independent decisions by weighing up pros and cons and gauging probabilities. Wanting to be independent means that a young person also wants *to be in control*. This can bring clashes with authority and, at the same time, an emerging *solidarity with friends* sometimes provokes uncharacteristic behaviour.

The inner meaning of *parables and proverbs* is now seen much more clearly. For example, the symbolism of a pearl would now come home. According to our guidelines, a two year old would simply have pronounced it 'Pretty'. A five year old may have added, 'It looks like one of Mummy's beads.' An eight year old, having learned how pearls develop, may have expressed sorrow for the oyster. The adolescent may agree with all these ideas, but could now appreciate that the oyster's pain had been eased and, at the same time, something of great value given in place of the original bit of grit.

Eventually, there could be even *deeper insight*, realising how a similar secret process could be at work in human beings, first soothing the pain and then bringing enrichment as a result of an unwelcome experience. Not all adolescents and adults are able to reason at this most advanced level. Intelligence and educational experience must play their part in the rate of progress. Sometimes, though, it is an experience of pain which itself opens the way to maturity.

Staying tuned

So there we have some guidance for starting to tune in to a child's level of understanding.

You may find it helpful to refer back to these guidelines when reading a relevant chapter to do with children's grief. Don't forget that children who are developmentally delayed and those who have been made more mature by experience are likely to have levels of understanding which differ from those suggested as being common amongst their age group, so prepare to be flexible. Stereotypes amongst children are rare!

It is essential that adults listen attentively to children if they are to achieve a proper meeting of minds with them. The guidelines given here are like a series of wavelengths, useful to know about when trying to tune in to a particular child's way of thinking, but useless without first making contact and then staying tuned.

Points to remember about a child's mind:

*Early thinking is by *matching* with the risk of mismatching because the child *judges by appearances*.

*Then come the earliest efforts to make logical deductions, which are often skewed by the child's continuing *face-value judgment*.

*The ability to *reason more logically* and to engage in *abstract ideas* often arrives late. This means that *insight* can be late to arrive, too.

*Even quite young children, with their less cluttered minds, can state something obvious which older minds had not observed.

*Experience and intelligence will both accelerate understanding.

Helpful Bible passages:

1 Corinthians 13:11–13
Proverbs 22:6
Colossians 3:20,21

Further reading:

Helen Bee, *The developing child*, 6th. edn (New

York, HarperCollins College Publishers 1991).
John Bowlby, *Child care and the growth of love*, 2nd. edn (Harmondsworth, Penguin 1990).

3

Tuning in to mind and spirit

Before we move on, let me tell you a story about how a mother's loving intuition tuned in to help her young son. As it shows so well how a young mind unfolds, and how she helped to clarify the child's ideas with images he could understand, it gives a practical example for some of the theory we have just gone through.

Ideas about illness mature with time

Christopher was born with cystic fibrosis. This illness meant that he had to have physiotherapy and take tablets several times each day for the whole of his life and even so he would get repeated chest infections. His treatment had begun in infancy and, though he was told very simply what his illness was called, for the first few years he accepted it all as a matter of routine and asked no questions. (This was his 'me, here, now' stage.)

Between six and seven years old, though, he asked, 'Why don't my brothers have cystic fibrosis? Why is it only me who has to have physio and all these tablets?' (He was now matching, comparing and noting differences.)

His mother answered, 'When you began to be made inside my tummy, Chris, one or two of the little cells that came together to make a baby weren't feeling very well at the time. These were the cystic fibrosis cells. The cells that made David and James were having a good day when they made them. Some of your other cells, though, made you extra special, too.'

As Christopher's father was an ex-Army man, she added, 'The strongest soldier is always chosen to deal with the hardest things.' Chris smiled at this and squared his shoulders. 'Right, Mum,' he said. Soon after this, Christopher was very ill in hospital, causing much anxiety. He had clearly observed this, as some weeks later, now about eight years old, he suddenly said, 'Mummy, am I going to die because of my cough? Will cystic fibrosis kill me?'

'What do you think, Chris?' asked his wise mother, trying to clarify how deeply he was thinking so that she could tune in at the right level.

'I don't really know what to think. Everyone seemed so worried when I was in hospital. People die in hospital, don't they? I don't want to die, Mum.'

'Well, Chris, every person born has to die sometime. You are right to say you don't know whether you will die from your cough because only God knows when someone will die. Some people die crossing the road and others live on even when they aren't expected to get better. Cystic fibrosis can be dangerous, but it can be helped.'

'What happens when you die, Mum? It must be horrible to be put in a big, dark hole all by yourself. You'd be cold and hungry and then all the worms would come and eat you up.' (Even at eight he still thought that a dead body would have feelings.)

'Is that what's been worrying you, Chris?'

'Yes, it is, Mum.'

'I'm only your mum, Chris, and I can't give you definite answers because only God knows, but I can tell you what I believe happens.'

Christopher loved butterflies, so she asked him to tell her what he knew about their beginnings. He told about the caterpillar and how it turns into a 'crystal list' before at last, 'It comes out of its brown, crunchy overcoat but this time it's a lovely butterfly that flies up towards the sunshine. If you try and catch it you never can.'

'Well, Chris, what you have just told me is what I believe happens when a person dies. When someone stops breathing, the time has come for them to change, just like the chrysalis changes into the butterfly. The part of us that changes is very special and important. It's the bit that tells us why we love someone or feel sorry about something.

'That part, Chris, never dies and lives for ever

in a world where there is only love and peace. That's where Grandpa is now, waiting for anyone else in his family to come there, too.'

Christopher's mother linked death to an ongoing relationship with someone well-known and also much loved. Other parents would find similarly dear names to mention, including that of Jesus, the dearest friend of all. Each parent will know, as Christopher's mother did, whom it would be natural to speak of as someone already known and special who could also be waiting to provide a welcome.

She then went on, 'The other part, like the chrysalis, is our body, which we don't need anymore. It's just like an old overcoat that we've outgrown and it's buried in the ground.' (Matching again!)

'The person who used to be inside has changed and isn't being buried, so they don't feel all those things like being alone or cold or hungry. To die is to change, Chris. It's the end of one sort of living and the start of another kind that lasts for ever. It isn't something to be frightened of. You will never be alone.'

'Thanks, Mum!' said Christopher, his previously worried face now changed to a sunbeam.

His mother still recalls that look of relief. After that, if he saw a funeral on the television, Chris would say, 'I suppose really the relatives are crying because they're going to miss the dead person, but the person that has died is still alive, but in a better place.'

When I saw Christopher next, he looked much better than he had done for some time. His anxiety had made his wheezy chest worse so to relieve the one had greatly helped the other.

There is no need to have done a full course in child development to get the answers right. Knowing and loving the child, listening with the inner ear and honestly trying hard to tune in – all these are the best preparations possible if difficult questions are to be met bravely and answers found that will meet the need. Christians also have access to the heavenly wisdom of the Father who designed young minds.

Many an 'SOS' prayer has been answered as a parent has tried to help a troubled child make sense of what is happening and then has felt inspired, as Christopher's mother was, to find ideas that exactly match the child's level of understanding and so relieve the tension.

A deep concern for many Christians will be to help a child into a personal relationship with the Lord Jesus. We need again to realise that young children will be unable to absorb concepts which to many adults have almost become articles of faith. As well as relying on the promptings of the Holy Spirit, we also need to tune in to a child's level of understanding just as we would do if teaching about anything else.

Growth in spiritual understanding

As you read on and hear about children with different levels of spiritual understanding, you may also like to look back at the guidelines in chapter 2 and see how the grasp of a spiritual truth often matches up with the child's likely way of looking at things in general. Even so, spiritual awareness should not be confused with intelligence.

The wonderful way in which our heavenly Father has designed children is that, from the start, loving relationships are so important to them. As they are also important to him, he is likely to use this route as the earliest pathway for communicating himself to them. Lessons that will come later include learning how he is the one who is truly high and mighty, as well as hearing in greater depth of all that he has done for us.

Trust

Even if they are not taught this at home some children, introduced to the idea at school or Sunday School, tune in eagerly to the idea of trusting the Lord Jesus to be with them all the time as the best of invisible friends.

To talk to a child of pre- and primary school age about 'asking Jesus into your heart' could be very confusing, as the heart will be known as 'the thing that thumps inside your chest'. To have Jesus as a constant but unseen friend is a much more comfortable and comforting notion. Our Lord's stated desire was for children simply to be allowed to come to him, and many do so.

After her first day at school, Alice, aged four, reported that she had been happy all morning but,

'I cried a bit at lunchtime.' One of the dinner ladies had shouted at the children, 'and I was a bit frightened'.

'So what did you do about it, Alice?' asked her concerned mother.

'Well, I knew that Jesus was with me, so I talked to him about it. He really was there, Mummy, so then I was all right again.' Already, Alice knew where to turn with her troubled feelings.

Saying 'Sorry'

Because relationships matter so much to them, children are quickly aware when there is a rift. To own up and say 'Sorry' to each other becomes the learned way of dispelling clouds.

Once, in over-excited mood, Alice had been rude to her father and was taken off for a walk by her mother.

'I didn't say "Sorry" to Daddy,' she remarked after a short silence.

'No,' said her mother, 'I noticed. How do you think Jesus feels about that?'

Alice was quick to realise that he was probably sad about it as she knew that he did not like rudeness. On their return, she produced a pretty white stone and, giving it to her father said, 'I do love you, Daddy, and I'm sorry.' Repentance brought forgiveness, sealed by a glad hug.

Such an experience can be used as a model to show how doing wrong hurts Jesus, our best friend and doing right makes us both happy. It could be matched up, too, with the Bible story of the father who welcomed home his wandering son (Luke 15). To be truly sorry and to tell the Lord Jesus so is the way to find the uncomfortable barrier taken away and openness and love restored.

Such love

As ideas of fairness and unfairness arise, the idea of deliberate selfishness is learned as well. By now, 'Sorry' has had to be said rather often. Deliberate disobedience will also have had uneasy consequences. Being sorry on behalf of others is also beginning.

An eight year old with this level of understanding came home from school sobbing, after hearing the Easter story, and said, 'Why do we call it *Good* Friday when what happened was so *bad*?' An answer couched in religious language could have been dutifully repeated but not properly comprehended. By now, though, she could grasp the explanation that what happened on Good Friday was how the Lord Jesus chose to help all the people (including her) who have not said 'Sorry' for doing wrong, even that awful wrong of killing him. Wrongdoing puts a barrier between us and God, but his love is so great that Jesus was willing to take the blame instead of us. He will forgive all those who love him enough to say how truly sorry they are and to thank him for his love. Then the joy of Easter Sunday can be theirs as well, as that wretched barrier comes down.

A child at this stage, able to compare and contrast her own best and worst behaviour, would now be able to make her own response and to say, 'Because Jesus loves me so much, I love him. I do want to please him, but I know that I also like to have my own way. I'll always need his help and lots more forgiveness before I learn to do what pleases him best.' In time, the word 'spirit' will be known to have good as well as its more popular spooky associations. There can then be more understanding of the work of the Holy Spirit, both nudging us when we do wrong and helping us to do right.

Sharing faith

It does not take intelligence to share faith. I once looked after a little boy who needed special education for his learning difficulties and epilepsy. When he was eleven years old, his father told me of their long struggle before finding a Sunday School to accept the boy and even now his father was asked to go, too.

At this point in the conversation, Philip came up to me, took my hand and said most earnestly, 'Doctor, please listen to me. Jesus died. Jesus loves you. Christ died for our sins.' He then repeated John 3:16 with reasonable accuracy. He was so pleased (and his father so relieved!) when I said how wonderful this all was and that I knew and trusted the Lord Jesus as well.

Counting the cost of personal commitment

Growing insight and awareness of what others will think can make it harder for teenagers to speak openly about matters of faith. It is now possible to weigh up the pros and cons of making a commitment to love and serve the Lord Jesus or deciding to go along with those who do not care about him. To think these things through and to make a decision after counting the cost should be the serious business of both adolescence and adulthood. To act as a channel for the Holy Spirit's fruitfulness is by now a recognisable ideal, but other tempting ambitions or consuming interests may beckon as well.

Teenagers who once professed to follow the Lord Jesus may break off contact with other Christians as they become more independent of their families and join in activities with a group of their own age. Only God knows whether they have really opted out or whether, behind the show of independence, the old bonds still hold.

Sometimes it is when a special personal relationship comes under threat that a longing arises for the security of a deep, lasting relationship with God. This may be for the first time or as an updating of the discarded views of childhood. It is not always spoken of or made obvious and older believers, knowing nothing about it, may remain very concerned about the spiritual standing of their young people.

At such times, we may simply have to pray on, not preaching but simply loving and listening. We look only on the outside. Our loving Lord looks on the heart. His judgment is entirely fair and entirely merciful. His Holy Spirit is well able to keep on communicating love and faithfulness. We sometimes have to take our hands off and trust the outcome entirely to him.

As I finished this chapter I spoke to Christopher's mother again. He had died two years before, at the age of eighteen. His mother told me of the growth in spiritual understanding that they had both experienced during his long illness and how, towards the end, he had spoken confidently of eternal life.

As a symbol of his entry into the new life which they had talked of together all those years ago, a butterfly is now carved onto the headstone of his grave. His soldier spirit has soared into freedom. The pain and the struggle are now with those he has left behind, yet the same hope is theirs, too.

Points to remember about spiritual growth:

*Trust in another is the foundation on which all further growth will depend.

*An experience of firm and fair love in action develops a pattern of unclouded responsiveness, then of rifts repented of and forgiven, and the joy of restored relationship. An *experience* of renewed 'at-one-ment' comes years before a child can grasp the *idea* of atonement.

*Under-sevens often have unseen, imaginary friends, but match information about God and Jesus with their experience of real, human love.

*Increased knowledge brings richer imagination. Junior school children can act with real altruism,

often as a group. Faith is shown by works.
*Exposure to new minds and growth into abstract thought can together bring ideas which challenge old creeds.
*It is possible for spiritual growth to become arrested at any of these stages.
*Search for a deeper faith may go on – and on.
*Maturity in faith comes when both heart and mind are committed to someone or something believed to offer true meaning and purpose to life. For some, this can be a political party or a cult.
*The Holy Spirit of God can so work in a life that this final commitment is one which owns Jesus as Lord. A little child could say these words without realising their full implications, but would then need wise and prayerful guidance to maintain growth towards maturity.
*Spiritual growth never ends!

Helpful Bible passages:
1 Corinthians 15:35–44
Ephesians 4:14–16
Luke 10:21

Further reading:

Francis Bridger, *Children finding faith* (London, Scripture Union 1988; to be reprinted).
Janet Gaukroger, *Sharing Jesus with under-fives* (Nottingham, Crossway Books 1994).
John Inchley, *Realities of childhood* (London,

Scripture Union 1986; now out of print).
Brian Wakeman, *Personal, social and moral education. A source book* (Tring, Lion Publishing 1984; now out of print).
John White, *Parents in pain* (Leicester, Inter Varsity Press 1979).

For children:

Patricia St. John, *Treasures of the snow* (London, Scripture Union, eleventh reprint 1992) Video version: International Films (Amersham, Scripture Press).
version: International Films (Amersham, Scripture Press).

4

Grieving infants and toddlers

If babies can be comforted, and we must all recognise that they can be, they must first have been distressed. When their crying is correctly interpreted by someone and the need met, the tears eventually cease.

If someone close to the baby has died, that need cannot be met. To recognise what effect this could have on the child we need to consider the making, as well as the breaking, of relationships in early infancy. Officially, infancy ends with the first birthday but this chapter will also be about those growing up into two year olds.

Attachment and loss: under one year old

All too often, we are likely to hear people referring even to a naked baby as 'it', as though the child were an object, not a person. In fact, healthy babies, born at term, can at once show great personal interest in other people through all five senses.

Babies are people, too

From birth, a baby likes to look most at a face. I have a lovely photograph of a baby called James, looking up at his mother and evidently studying her face when he was only fifteen hours old. He even smiled with pleasure as he did so. Within a week he would know her by smell and only a few weeks later he would show that he recognised her face and her voice out of a group. Babies are born ready to relate in a way which is unique within the animal world.

When relationships have been warm and close, a baby of only a few weeks old will give a great welcome back to special people. If they do not come back after an absence, the child's restlessness and crying, to be followed eventually by whimpering and withdrawal, are indicators that the infant is feeling bereft.

The worst loss for babies is to be parted from whoever has been closest to them, usually their mothers. In some parts of the world infants are looked after by a mother substitute, such as a grandmother or big sister. The closeness of the bond between them, like that developed with a nanny or other employed caregiver, is not always appreciated. The abrupt termination of such attachments for whatever cause should be recognised as a serious bereavement to the child.

How to help a bereft infant

The first need is to recognise that even new babies can feel bereaved. Because they cry so much for other reasons, their distress when someone dies may not be identified. This is especially so if everyone else in the family is coping with bereavement themselves. It can even be viewed as the last straw that the baby is constantly crying 'at a time like this'.

Before learning to play 'peek-a-boo', the child may not yet have been very sure that people who are out of sight are, in fact, still around. If the usual caregiver is no longer there to respond to a lonely infant's cries, the presence of some other familiar person may gradually restore the calm, though possibly not for days or weeks. For a time it may also be comforting to offer a scarf or garment which still smells of the one who has gone. As long as the child's needs are recognised and attempts made to meet them, time is likely to bring healing, especially if the rest of the familiar circle is tuned in and ready to close the gap.

Bereaved toddlers: one and two years old

The situation of loss is harder to deal with for an infant who is now well aware of other people's permanence. For someone special to disappear without any reappearance can be very distressing, especially if the child were then to be sent away to stay with someone not very well known.

The pain of sudden separation

Some years ago I went to work in Uganda and was shocked to see a look of total devastation on the faces of children between one and two years old. They were suffering from a particular kind of malnutrition called kwashiorkor, which includes amongst its symptoms terrible apathy and amongst its signs a hurt look in the eyes.

After careful enquiry we found that many of these previously breastfed infants had been sent away from their families, often miles from home, because their mothers had died. Others underwent this experience as a method of weaning. In either case, they did not know the reason as the adults did. It was clear that they felt grief, even if they did not know its cause. They had lost those they loved the best and in their misery refused to eat. Already malnourished, many of them died from added infection which they were too ill to fight. They repeatedly turned away from any attempt to comfort them. Their faces said it all.

Sudden death

A young mother found one of her three month old twins dead in the cot. In a panic, she tried to give her the 'kiss of life'. Twenty month old Amy saw this and ran round the house, screaming. Later, she would not accept the boy twin, calling instead for their dead sister. She was allowed to see the baby dressed for her funeral, then told that she had gone away. Mention of heaven, perhaps never heard about before, mystified her completely. She still ran round the house for weeks afterwards, calling the baby's name.

Calling death by its name

To call death by another name can be very confusing to young children. To speak of loss could imply that the one who is lost may one day be found. A child who was told that her dead brother had 'gone to sleep' had insomnia for weeks. Even a toddler knows when flowers or butterflies are dead, so 'dead' is the best word to use, however hard this can be for adults to say.

Seeing the body

Startling as this idea may seem to many people, it was good that Amy's parents allowed her to see her dead baby sister. She would need more than a brief glimpse, though, to take in the truth.

In these circumstances, it should first be said, gently but quite plainly, that the baby is dead. This means that she will not look or laugh any more and she will not move if touched. Older children may be helped by going over this first with a doll, but a toddler absorbs experience better than explanation. After this forewarning, to be taken in somebody's arms to see the dead baby properly, to touch her or hold her and so to see how quiet and unresponsive the body now is, would mean more to a very young child than a lot of words. It should be explained clearly that her unnatural stillness means that the baby is dead and time should be given for this to sink in. The implication that there will now be no return is not yet within a toddler's understanding. Because of this, the child does not share the agony felt by adults and there may not even be any tears at this stage.

The funeral

If she had been taken to the funeral, it would have been unlikely that Amy, still at the 'me, here, now' stage, would have picked up more than the sense that everyone was sad because the baby had died. It is unlikely, at twenty months of age, that she would have registered the significance of the small coffin.

Changed behaviour as a sign of grief

A child under two years old may show clear evidence of grief. Being very restless and uncooperative can be signs of the confusion which bereavement brings, whilst abnormal quiet or more marked withdrawal, sometimes with weight loss, can spell depression.

Because Amy would not yet have realised that death is irreversible, it was to be expected, even after having said her farewells, that she would still run round, as she did, looking for her dead sister. Hard as this must have been for them, her parents would have had to keep reminding her how she had been able to tell, when she saw her, that the baby was dead. She would not be coming back, which is why people now seemed so sad and sometimes cried.

After weeks of fruitless searching, she may have

become quieter, though still uneasy. As long as her parents' own grief was obvious, any further disturbances in Amy's behaviour would be more likely to reflect their tension than still being due to her own sorrow.

Visits to the cemetery can be very confusing for small children, especially if they have already been told that someone has gone to heaven. To take offerings of flowers or toys to put on a grave indicates to a young mind that the missing person is still able to enjoy them, so has not really gone away. If such visits are to be made, it is best for them to be explained as going to a place where those left behind can still think about the dead person. It is probable that a little child would find more help from a photograph album.

How to help a depressed infant or toddler

The needs of the twin boy in Amy's family could easily have been overlooked, but being the only baby now he would probably have had extra cuddles, which would themselves offer him personal comfort.

Extra personal attention will provide necessary reassurance to most little ones about still being loved and valued, though the sense of loss can still be puzzling and sad, even more so if a parent has died. The child's normal daily routine should be kept up, if this is possible, to avoid any further upset, although this can be hard for a disrupted family to remember to do.

Talking in terms of relationships

To try to explain about heaven at this stage can leave little ones quite bemused. Especially if heaven has never been heard of before, it would be better to say, gently and repeatedly, that the person is dead and will not be coming back. To children, the phrase 'up there' can mean being in an aeroplane or amongst the stars. It then adds hurt to hurt to be laughed at.

Yet the things that adults say will be believed, repeated and mulled over in an attempt to make sense of them. To link the dead person to an ongoing relationship can be most comforting, even if still baffling. Christian parents need not fear to say that the dead person is with the Lord Jesus when his is a loved and trusted name to their children, or to explain heaven as being the lovely but faraway place where he lives. Amy's cousin, a year older than herself, was cheered to think of the baby's having gone to join Shep, their dead sheepdog. That was her idea of heaven.

Wording can be important here. It is better not to say, 'Jesus has taken her away,' for who might he think of taking away next? It is much more acceptable to think of his 'taking care of' dead people than for them to have been suddenly removed, even by him.

When death comes more slowly

Many a new baby needs care for weeks in a highly technical unit. Adults sometimes need similar care, at some stage of an illness or after an accident.

Intensive care

Equipment which makes adults anxious holds no fears for little children. They simply do not understand it and may find it all very curious and even interesting, but not alarming. It is usually much less upsetting for them to see what is going on than to be made to feel left out.

Clara, aged four, was admitted unconscious after a head injury and put on to a life-support machine. In the upset, her two year old sister, Carol, was sent to stay with an aunt so it took some days to realise that she was sleeping badly and not at all her usual self. At home, she had shared a bed with Clara, so it was arranged for her to come and see her sister.

First, she looked at Clara quietly from her aunt's arms. She then wriggled down and tried repeatedly and rather crossly, but in vain, to wake her. Finally she asked to lie down beside her on the hospital bed, eyes tight shut and, it seemed, tried to deny the unfamiliar by recreating the familiar. No doubt still puzzled, she could tell that Clara was no longer as she used to be. Later she attended the funeral, sharing in the family's farewell, but it took some months for her to get back to her usual self.

Terminal care

When death comes more slowly still, little children can safely be included in taking care of a dying member of the family, even if this is only sitting on the bed for company, or holding hands. It helps them to pick up the idea that a change is coming.

There are no more walks or even many chats together now and the dying person may be very sleepy.

A child of this age has very limited understanding about time, so too much forewarning is not going to be helpful. It is better to stay involved as much as the dying person can bear, and to say goodbye at the end. The grief to follow will still be real but, being less obvious in expression than after a sudden loss, can more easily be overlooked.

Infants in outlook though older in years

There are many children whose understanding remains very simple whatever their age in years. It would be a mistake to think that they do not grieve when someone dear to them dies.

Claire, aged six and a half, shared a bedroom with her two year old brother Jimmy. Both children were seriously delayed in development and neither of them could sit up or speak, but could always be heard 'chatting' and giggling together early in the morning. One day, Claire's voice got louder and louder, but with no response from Jimmy. He had died in the night.

Claire's parents wanted to let her see what had happened and so put her into Jimmy's cot, but she only turned towards his body, as she had always turned to him, and laughed. However, for some weeks afterwards she was noticeably much quieter both at home and at school. Whenever Jimmy's name was mentioned, the little girl turned her head with an expectant smile and then seemed sad not to see him.

'So what did you do about it?' I asked her mother. 'Well, we hadn't got Jimmy so we gave her more attention. I also talked to her about him and explained what had happened. Although she wouldn't understand the words, I'm sure she picked up the love and concern and sympathy and she slowly got back to her old self.' It would have been all too easy to leave this little girl's grief unrecognised and unmet by assuming that she could not understand. It does not take intelligence to love, or to be sad when a loved one disappears.

Keeping the memory green

Because little children do not realise that death is permanent, the need to keep on repeating the painful truth to them is hard, but can eventually help everyone, old and young, to face the truth.

At the same time, starting to make mention of the loved one's name in a happier context, remembering shared experiences or looking through the photograph album together, can help everyone slowly to come to terms with the loss.

Even a two year old can hold memories for a long time. One child of this age who had kissed her dead sister goodnight for the last time surprised her mother a year later when she had to take an antibiotic and correctly remarked that it was the same medicine as her sister used to take.

Sometimes parents worry about such long

remembered involvement with someone who has died, but most see it as a cause for gratitude. They themselves will never forget and it is good when even little ones keep on mentioning a loved name with affection.

It is even better when all those left behind know the comfort of an ongoing relationship with the Lord Jesus. He still links together the seen and the unseen members of a family with a love that has itself been to the greatest depths. His love will never fail to keep reaching out to all who have loved and lost.

Points to remember for infants and toddlers:

*Even a baby can feel bereft.

*To be cut off from a loved one feels the same as being rejected.

*Seeing a dead body is less fearful than it can be for adults.

*Grief can be expressed by searching or changed behaviour as well as by tears.

*Memories last for a long time.

Helpful Bible passages:

Mark 10:13–16

Isaiah 40:11

Further reading:

John Bowlby, *Attachment and loss* (Harmondsworth, Penguin Books Ltd 1969).

Marshall H Klaus and John J Kennell, *Maternal-infant bonding* (St Louis, The CV Mosby Company 1976).

Janet Goodall, '*A social score for kwashiorkor: explaining the look in the child's eyes*', in Developmental Medicine and Child Neurology *21*;(1974), pp.374–384.

Nancy Kohner with Jenni Thomas, *Grieving after the death of your baby* (Bourne End, Professional Care Productions 1993).

Neville Smith, *Miscarriage, stillbirth and neonatal death* (London, The Churches' Committee for Hospital Chaplaincies 1993).

5

Infants and toddlers who die

Babies are people, too, so dying babies have personal needs. What are their needs? Could our adult minds as easily fail to meet them as we must sometimes fail their brothers and sisters at the time of a death in the family?

Babies who die within their first few weeks

By far the greatest number of babies who die do so within a month of their birth, most commonly because they have been born too soon or too small. Most of them die in hospital, often in a high-powered unit expressly designed to keep them alive. When I was a young doctor, no-one else but the professional team was allowed in. As time went by, it was realised that for infants to survive at all and then later to fit in easily to family life, they needed personal as well as professional care.

Babies need love in order to live

As we saw in the last chapter, babies are born ready to relate. This is such a lovely reminder of one of the marks of God's image in us, that he has designed us to find joy in personal relationships right from the start. Without such caring and personal input, a baby can die. The only time when life is not worth living is when it is being endured without love.

Knowing this, any up-to-date unit providing intensive neonatal care now encourages parents and new babies to get to know each other, even when the baby is sick. Eyes can meet, voices can be heard and even cuddles can be managed when a child is still cooped up in an incubator. If the baby is very ill, nobody really knows how many of these messages are received but it helps parents to be able to offer them.

Tender, loving care right to the end

When an infant on such a unit is dying and there is no more hope of recovery, equipment is usually removed so that the baby's last moments can be spent comfortably in the parents' arms. If desired, other members of the family, or a pastoral minister, can be there, too. Dying babies may only be hours old, but can still be treated with tender, personal care.

The same principle holds if a baby has a serious disability which is going to make life short. It may be decided, after thorough assessment, that all necessary care can be given at home if the family is ready. Failing this, hospital should be made as homelike as possible.

In a baby's terms, care means being made comfortable, with interested people to listen to, to gaze at and to be cuddled by. This teaches infants very quickly how to show a pleased response to personal love.

Such practice still does not happen worldwide. Some parents feel unable to face caring for a child who is going to die or who will remain very disabled. This is often the first reaction of grief and could change, given time and support. Some of the saddest faces I have ever seen have been those of children in Eastern European institutions, abandoned there sometimes only because of disfigurement and rarely, if ever, visited by their families.

Death by about two years old

Except for the newly born and those with a lingering disability, children who die during their first two years tend to do so suddenly, from an overwhelming infection or serious accident. Each kind of death means a special kind of grief for the onlookers, but the sufferer has needs, too, which are easy to overlook.

The sudden approach of death

By now, family feeling is usually well established. If in hospital and conscious, an infant can be almost as distressed by loneliness as by all else that is happening. In the crisis, many strangers come and go and do new and unpleasant things to a child who has probably never left home before. Infants can have no idea that all that they endure is intended to save their lives.

To have someone familiar staying alongside (not just in the waiting room) remains very important, even though that person, too, may be upset and uncertain. Although for a nearly two year old it must be very bewildering that parents do not put a stop to these activities, a conscious child could feel altogether deserted without their reassuring voices and cuddles. Early childhood is a time for receiving many unexpected hurts and to be kissed better is a sign of continuing love even when it can no longer offer a complete remedy.

Children in this age group live life hour by hour and even tomorrow can seem unimaginably far away. Whenever possible, keeping up with familiarity, ranging from special toys to prayer times, gives back a semblance of normality in the midst of so much that is abnormal.

Things go from bad to worse

If instead of there being a good response the threat of death looms larger, the child's awareness is mercifully likely to be failing. If a life support machine is in use, close physical contact is harder to maintain. Even so, there is some evidence that familiar voices (and favourite music) can still get through.

When it is clear that the battle is being lost, the family would be included in the decision to withdraw any kind of mechanical life support.

They may also be asked to decide about the donation of organs. Time would be given to bring in others to support, to say last farewells and then to make a final prayerful commitment before leaving the unit.

The staff on these highly technical units feel a particular sense of sadness when children die and a child's special nurse may value being included when the final prayers are offered. The unconscious witness of a Christian family, even when very distressed, can have a lasting effect on those who see many others facing death bitterly and without hope.

Death comes more slowly

Recognition that a child is slowly dying may come after an immediate crisis is over but without any more recovery to follow, as after a head injury. Alternatively, the prospect of an early death may have been looming for much of a child's life. It is part of the merciful protection, given in the heavenly Father's design for their minds, that little ones have no sharp awareness of impending death.

Finding comfort in caring

Grief can be so terrible that it can take a long time for parents to see that another aspect of God's mercy and pity unfolds as they care for their own dying infants. Our Lord's concern for creativity in human relationships lasts right up to the point when death seems to come in and destroy them.

It is through these final acts of loving tenderness

that many a family's deep seated grief has found a grain of consolation. Love outlasts life itself when God's intention for mutual tender, loving care is finally fulfilled. In time, the commitment shown in the face of pain may affect a wider circle still.

It is this pattern which emerges clearly in *Love and loss*, a study reported from the centre where I used to work during years in which a hospital policy altered completely. Initially, the professional mode of practice discouraged much personal involvement between parents and their dying babies. Over time, this changed to a policy which fully encouraged this, right to the end.

Conversations took place with eighty parents, each having lost a baby with a major spinal defect (spina bifida) too extensive for surgery. All the children had died within a year of birth, but there were striking differences reported by parents whose experiences had also been very different.

At the start of the period under review, no babies had ever gone home and not all were even visited by their families. Eventually, a Christian family decided to take their little boy home to nurse him there themselves until he died. This was the turning point. They shared their experience with another family whose baby, David, had spina bifida and was under my care so I could see for myself what happened. They took David home, where he died a few months later after a brief but mostly contented life.

By the end of the survey, very few babies living for over a week with this severe type of inoperable disability stayed on in the hospital. Years later, the parents whose babies had gone home believed that they had enjoyed a better life and that relationships within their families had become closer. Those whose infants had been left in hospital often described their babies' lives as having been 'rotten'. In contrast, the children who were cared for at home tended to live longer.

Here we come to see the heavenly Father's touch. When babies had gone home, their parents' own sadness had been softened by providing for their care. Short lives, lived in utter frailty, had still been capable of love and influence. Babies do not look ahead and worry. Even a short life can be sweet and will be made much sweeter by personal care. As one mother in our survey commented, 'It was love that kept her alive.' From the way that she spoke, it was clear that love had endured up to the end, and beyond.

Terminal care for infants

Some disabled or chronically ill children will have longer lives than others, but the principle of continuing care remains the same. At this age, only one idea at a time holds close attention, so that the mind can often be distracted from the illness by having things and people to play with. Thinking about something else helps to relieve milder discomforts. Such distractions can be simply watching other children play, or looking at nearby mobiles or pictures. If there comes a time when discomfort gets so bad that it is spoiling life, there are plenty of helpful medicines to choose from. Giving powerful drugs, even morphine or heroin, to a dying child is designed not 'to put him out' but to relieve distress. Children of all ages usually tolerate these medicines well in the right dosage, without becoming very drowsy. Giving them round the clock is what keeps discomfort away, rather than allowing it to peak and so causing distress all over again.

Encouraging all the children in the family to spend time with each other helps the well ones to see for themselves what is happening and can also cheer up the ill one. Hours of television are no substitute for the personal touch. A loving presence, even intermittently, makes all the difference to life's enjoyment, from start to finish.

Coming and going to and from hospital and all that can go with this, including repeated operations, may have become very familiar to the family of a disabled or chronically ill child. So far this has always ended up in going home again.

During what can have been long and hard experiences for the child, the family and also their professional supporters, keeping up healthy, helpful and honest relationships should ideally have remained a priority. As Joni Eareckson Tada discusses in her book, *When is it right to die?*, they can in time be the pivot on which important decisions swing. In the care of little children, such decisions finally have to be made by others acting on their behalf, so it is vital that a particular infant's way of looking at life is kept well in mind. When this is done sensitively, the child, too, has played an important part in balancing the decisive judgment. It is never right to decide to kill a dying child, but it can be right to decide that some forms of life saving therapy are now going to be futile, so should be stopped.

Freddie was just under eighteen months old on the day that he died. He had been born with such a badly twisted spine that it was likely, as he grew, to cause paralysis of his legs. It was decided to operate at our local specialist hospital forty miles from his home. Visits from his parents and sister were faithfully kept up but only with great difficulty.

One operation led to another but did not stop the advent of paralysis. Freddie was in hospital for months. We all loved him, but were increasingly worried about his recurrent and severe chest infections. These were made more serious because of his persistently crooked back.

Freddie's condition was incurable and getting steadily worse. His survival, even in the short term, would depend on machinery which would keep him immobilised and unconscious. There was no prospect of restoring him to family life. To keep on with this kind of existence was prolonging dying, not enriching living.

As the chest infection grew worse despite antibiotics, everyone agreed that, as it could not helpfully prolong his life, artificial respiration should not be used again. Instead, all our care was turned towards making Freddie as comfortable as possible. His mother later said how, on the last morning, he gave up the struggle and 'he himself decided to go to our Lord.' He died at rest in her arms, the place denied to them both for months.

The sheet anchor

It is intensely and unspeakably painful to lose a child whose life is only just beginning and whose promise will be unfulfilled. If our Lord wept when his friend Lazarus died, our own scorching tears are surely appropriate for such a loss as this.

The sheet anchor has to be the certainty of our heavenly Father's love. Having designed us to be committed to loving relationships with each other, his own loving relationship with us undergirds all the others. He will help each one involved, little children included, to hold on to him day by day, despite the dreadful pain of parting. He can also be trusted to continue to care for the one who has gone.

Points to remember for children up to about two years old:

*It is hard to hold two things firmly in mind at once.

*Distraction can overcome some discomforts.

*When strange people do strange things, familiarity brings contentment.

*If a time comes to stop curative therapy, there is always something else to offer, including tender loving care.

*Ethical dilemmas in care can sometimes be resolved in a context of creative relationships.

Helpful Bible passages:
Genesis 1:27
Mark 9:36,37
Deuteronomy 31:8
Isaiah 65:17–23

Further reading:

Joni Eareckson Tada, *When is it right to die? Euthanasia on trial* (London, Marshall Pickering 1992).

Eileen Delight and Janet Goodall, *Love and loss: conversations with parents of babies with spina bifida managed without surgery,* 1971–1981 (London, MacKeith Press 1990).

John Wyatt and Andrew Spencer, *Survival of the weakest. A Christian approach to extreme prematurity* (London, Christian Medical Fellowship 1992).

6

Someone is slowly dying: helping 3–7 year olds

It is such fun to splash paint around at the play-group. A little child must wonder why all this effort meets with such admiration there, yet can cause so much fuss when it has been quietly redirected into helping Daddy with the new decorations at home. It takes time and many bruised feelings to sort out how to do only what adults like best.

It is confusing to be a learner

This is the age for matching up ideas but also for mismatching. Thus, if adults are upset, children can think that this is due to their own behaviour rather than there being some other cause to account for it. Reasoning step by step comes later.

Words mean what I want them to mean

A boy of three years old had a phobia about lumps following his brother's death from 'a lump in his tummy'. He had to be told that there were good lumps, too. This verbal message was then backed up by the visual aid of sugar lumps. Yet an out-of-the-ordinary word, such as leukaemia, could have been accepted and used as the name for what was wrong with someone (even with himself) without any alarm bells being sounded. It would not have had other associations.

It is easy to think that a child who can repeat a phrase really understands it. Often the words are simply being repeated parrot-fashion. Yet a quotation can sometimes be useful to a young child when trying to explain the inexplicable.

Emma was four years old when asked by her friends, 'Why did your brother die?' She replied, 'He had cancer of his back.' This explanation was accepted by the others without question and satisfactorily stopped the prevailing rumour that he had choked to death in his own blood. Yet when asked by an adult what cancer of the back meant to her, she could not explain it further. She had been involved in Marc's terminal care and death at home, so she was not ignorant about what had happened. Her problem lay in putting it into words. To quote what she had heard someone else say provided a ready-made answer.

True or false?

Sorting out fact from fiction can be genuinely dif-

ficult at this stage of life. The imagination is rich and fantastic and is constantly being fed with amazing new impressions, which do not only come from video and television. As cause and effect are not yet properly understood, many things (such as going up in a lift) must seem quite magical and others (such as zooming down again) very alarming.

Adults may frown about children telling lies, or living in a world of their own, and of course part of growing up is learning to sort out reality from unreality. Yet part of being very young is for fact and fancy to keep getting muddled up. Under five years old, children may not realise that dreams go on only inside the head and day dreams, too, may seem very real. It can be hard to be asked for a straightforward account of something. It can also be hard sometimes to have a clear view of what is going on.

Facing someone else's death

Forty per cent of children under five years old believe that death is reversible, a belief strengthened by certain popular cartoons in which a character can be flattened by a steamroller in one sequence and come back as bouncy as ever in the next. They are unlikely to register the information that someone is dying until there is something relevant to see. To forewarn a child of this age too soon will either not mean very much or overstimulate the imagination. Yet there must be some paving of the way for a child who is eventually to experience the painful loss of someone greatly loved.

Death comes closer

It is better to let a young child's life go on as normally as possible for as long as possible when there is a long illness to be faced within the family. Interference with routine should at first be given short-term explanations. 'Daddy has to stay off work for a time as he has to have some special treatment to make him feel a bit stronger.' More will need to be said later on.

Sowing seed thoughts

The mindset of the young child still centres things back on to self and is also used to being blamed, confused and otherwise in trouble. Any mysterious comings and goings of a loved one can be misinterpreted, as can other people's mood swings. The child can feel somehow personally responsible for these and may draw fantastic private conclusions.

It is wiser for adults to say truthfully what is going on, yet without needing to tell all. Small people have big ears and if not in the know can pick up worrying ideas. To overhear, 'I fear we're going to lose her,' could result in a small boy's gluing himself to his mother to stop her getting lost and thereby giving her no rest at all. On the other hand, to have it openly stated that Mummy is not very well and needs to stay quiet gives an inkling that things are not as they were but she is still here.

Explanations should match up

Because this is the age for matching things together, an explanation offered in terms of, 'It is (or is not) like . . .' is always a great help. 'It is like when you were sick and wanted to stay in bed. Granny feels tired and sick, too, so we won't stay long today.' 'Daddy's nosebleeds aren't the same as yours because we can stop yours quickly, but he has an illness called leukaemia and it's part of that.'

It can come as a surprise to grown-ups, who may be dreading the next question, to find that it does not necessarily come and that even lame attempts at explanation have been perfectly acceptable. This is because the data is being processed by the child, matching it up as suggested. When this has been done, another query may arise (though it may not always be posed at a very convenient time!) It is not easy for adults to stay constantly tuned, but a wise rule is to take one question at a time and answer it simply but honestly.

A child's questions need to be clarified

As young children cannot always connect their thoughts very well, their own meaning may not always be clear. Fortunately, they are likely to ask again if not satisfied with the first answer. To ask a child, 'I wonder why you're asking me that?' can help to clarify an odd query and also gives more time to think up the best reply.

It is important to stay truthful in these exchanges. If adults cannot be relied upon to tell the truth, fact and fiction will remain confused for children, too. It is not possible to anticipate all a child's questions and to some the answer may well be, 'I don't know', or, 'I'll have to think about that.'

Even if a dreaded question should come, its implications are not yet likely to be fully understood. What lies behind an apparently straightforward query such as, 'When is Daddy going to get well?' should still be clarified before giving a straight answer. The child may merely be asking whether Daddy will be well in time to go on holiday. If, though, there seems to be more to it than that, it would be fair to say, 'I'm afraid it looks as if he's never going to be well enough to take you out on the bike any more. But at least that means that we've got him at home with us.'

Telling the truth in stages

It is good to remember that truth can be told in stages, each statement to be built on later. To tell too much too soon, or to tell untruths, can bring great bewilderment.

For a small child to be told the name of someone's disorder, be this cancer, AIDS or Alzheimer's disease, but to be asked to keep it a secret, is probably too much to hope for. To overhear such names, though, would as yet mean very little. As long as the social stigma of AIDS persists, it is probably best simply to say, 'Tom has an infection of his blood, so if his nose bleeds we'll put on plastic gloves to clean it up. Otherwise we treat him just the same.'

A greater problem for children of this age will be the changes in personality, including loss of memory, which may develop as certain diseases advance. It can be a great relief to hear, 'Granny's like this because she's so ill now, not because she doesn't love us any more.'

Some may feel it better, particularly for a bright child, to name the disease openly but to say that this is only mentioned within the family or by a doctor. 'A lot of people would be afraid that they might catch his infection just by being with Tom. That's not true, but if they knew about it they might stop being friends so it is better not to worry them. It matters a lot to Tom that we know and we want to take care of him.'

Looking ahead

Ahead of time, a wise family will seize opportunities to discuss, in as matter of fact a way as they can, what dying, death and funerals are like. Openings could arise naturally, for example by the timely death of a pet or, more often, by keeping a careful watch on television news programmes. There is no need to link the topic directly with the person who is ill, but talking the ideas over will give a foundation to be built on later.

Only when her brother's condition started more obviously to get worse was four year old Emma told that Marc was very poorly. She already knew that he had cancer and what she could already see for herself was gently but clearly pointed out. His legs had given way and he could only see with one eye. Although he was in bed a lot now, he could still fill his room with pictures, scribble in his notebook and enjoy being with his family and friends.

After some weeks, Emma's mother told her that Marc was not going to get any better. Her older sister knew already that he was going to die. This was a Christian family, so the girls were told that he would be going to heaven to be with the Lord Jesus. Death was also described to them in terms which even young Emma could grasp. 'It's a bit like a snail leaving its shell, or someone going on a journey to start living in a new place.' Marc was about to move out. Just as the snail leaves its shell behind, or people move into a different house, so he would leave his body behind and go away. This would be sad for them because they would no longer see him, but he would be with Grandad as well as with the Lord Jesus, so it would be lovely for him after being so ill for so long.

Ideas like these must not be blithely handed out to other children without knowing their background. Comparisons must match experience if they are to ring true. (See also page 107.) Whatever else helps, it is always comforting to think of the dead person's being with someone else whose name is dear to the family. Ongoing relationships link past, present and future when farewells have to be said in the here and now.

Saying goodbye

After Marc's death, their father brought the two girls home from school to see for themselves what had happened. Although Marc's 'shell' was still there, they reported later, 'It was like he'd moved out. He was peaceful and it looked like he was asleep, but we knew he wasn't just asleep.' The door of his room was left ajar and they each went in and out as they wished, sitting there for some time, letting the truth sink in. As their father reported afterwards, 'They held his hand and everything seemed so natural. We were really pleased about it.'

These parents wisely did not rush to have Marc's body removed for several hours so that they could all spend time in this way, both individually and together. There could be no doubt and no room for fantasy. He was no longer breathing, did not respond when spoken to and slowly began to feel colder to the touch. Their dear Marc was dead. He had moved out and, they believed, moved on.

Such sensitivity allowed the girls to go at their own pace and helped their parents, too, to prepare for each next step as they spoke of it together.

Giving children the choice

Marc's sisters were given freedom to choose whether they saw his body or not, but were also told that they need not be afraid to do so. Where there is genuine doubt about how appropriate it is for children to do this, it could be a useful rule of thumb that they are likely to find it most helpful to say goodbye in person to the body of someone it would previously have been natural for them to see in bed, even if this never happened.

A mother whose son had died told me how, as a young child, she had been forced against her will to go in and kiss her cold and dead uncle goodbye. Now she had found it impossible to do the same thing for her own son. She had not been particularly close to the uncle and would have preferred to have been left on the sidelines after his death, much as she had been during his life. She allowed her own children to choose for themselves whether or not to see their brother's body.

Given such a choice, it is often the older children or the adults in a family who decide against it. Though they can be afraid both of what they may see and of their own reactions, they should not be tempted to dissuade the younger ones, who see things so differently.

Normally there are a few days in which to make final decisions before the day of the funeral. As things are at present, though, when someone dies from certain infectious diseases, including AIDS, once death has been certified the body is removed in a special bag. No-one is then permitted to see or touch it again, though sometimes the undertaker will allow a final glimpse of the dead person's face. Such farewells are accordingly said all too quickly.

Seeing can be both believing and grieving

It is, of course, important that such a special experience is conducted sensitively. It is best first to talk about 'going to say goodbye to Auntie,' rather than of 'going to see Auntie's body.' Children rarely see the bodies of most adults except on a beach and would find this a most peculiar idea. The child should be told to expect the person to be much the same to look at as before, but now very still and unresponsive. Someone familiar should offer a hand to hold as they go in to the room together.

The child's first reaction may be to stare hard at the body rather than to express emotion, or perhaps to ask questions about the clothing or bedding, or why the person is so still. The points made beforehand are now made again to help the strange lack of response to sink in. Each child is different and behaviour will vary. If tears come, they should be allowed to flow. The child may want to snuggle up close to the dead person, or more rarely may start to scream. Hard as any of these reactions is to witness, the child will need a cuddle but need not be rushed away. More than one return visit may be needed before going, as it should be known, for the last goodbye. The whole delicate operation is one of sensitive tuning in to the child's needs and responses, not one to be rigidly controlled by what the adults think ought to happen.

A six year old Albanian boy, who had watched his mother dying slowly over a period of eighteen months, was still without insight about her serious condition when she died in hospital. He had a brief and shocking glimpse of her body just before the funeral after which he screamed and cried constantly. For the next six months he refused to speak to his father, attributing the death to him, and for four years moved in with his grandparents before finally going back home. Six years later he had become a strikingly tenderhearted boy. At a holiday camp, he was the one to comfort distressed and homesick children. His own need of care seemed to have inspired him to care for others.

Other children have grown up resentful that they were sent away and never given a chance to say goodbye to someone who had been special to them. In contrast, Marc's father later wrote, 'It is frightening, looking back, that I could have insisted that the children did not see him, or attend the funeral. That would have been a tragic mistake.'

The funeral

(See also page 106.) It is all too easy for grown-ups to say, 'You won't want to come to the funeral', or even to send their children away without explanation whilst they hurry to get the ceremony over. Marc's parents arranged the service for a week after his death, by which time they had explained what was to happen and helped the children to choose whether or not to attend. Both Joanne and Emma decided that the family should all be together at this special farewell to Marc. They accordingly went to the church service and then to another at the crematorium, during which the coffin sank from view. They were fully attentive and without overwhelming distress.

It is a good idea to have someone not too closely involved sitting near the children. Although well briefed before his grandmother's funeral, one attentive three year old piped up in mid-service, 'But how did Granny get into the coffin?' He had sensibly been put to sit with his other grandfather who simply whispered that someone had put her into it after she was dead. At such a sad time for her, his grieving mother could have found this a difficult moment to handle.

After the funeral

It is not unusual for those left behind to have surprising difficulty in remembering what their loved one used to look like. Photographs can help or haunt, but children often like to have one. Immediately after her brother's death, Emma's teacher was very impressed by the way in which the four year old handled the various questions from her classmates about Marc's death and the funeral.

A year later she tried to tell me what she remembered. Now five years old, her recall improved as her older sister spoke of him, too. She told how she had overheard Marc asking if he was going to die and she also recalled how he had looked after his death. Her memories of the funeral and cremation were sketchy but untroubled. It was many years later that she said how puzzled she had been when, at that particular crematorium, the coffin went *down*, as Marc was supposed to be going *up* to heaven.

Significantly, the most animated part of her immediate recollections was of the joyful times the family had shared when they were all together before his death. Marc had loved elephants, and her idea of him in heaven was 'riding on a heleph-ant'. Emma still missed her brother, particularly during school holidays, but the tone of this conver-sation was sweet as much as sad.

Bereavement and how it shows itself

There is no escape from the fact that loss is painful, yet people are often surprised that young children may show such little evidence of open grief when someone dear to them dies. Clearly, this is not always so. Many things must make a difference, including the closeness of the previous bond and the child's personality, as well as the sensitivity with which it has been possible to ease the separ-ation by preparation and involvement.

Another influence which protects young children from experiencing the full sharpness of grief is the kindly way in which their minds have been fashioned by our heavenly Father. The full impli-cations of the parting are not yet understood, so the blow is thereby softened. Even so, for years, death is thought to be reversible and wishes are believed to be very powerful. This combination means that there is often a firm hope that the loved one will return. This can be strong enough to stem torrents of tears at the time, though they may come out later in life if the hurt has never been healed.

After the first impact, a young child's grief is so often reticent that, within days or weeks of a death in the close family, people may say, 'She's got over it now,' or, 'He's too little to understand what's happened.' Such remarks are based on the false idea that young children will show their feelings in an adult way.

Guilty withdrawal

The quiet child who has so quickly 'got over it' or is 'being so good' may actually be suffering from a sense of responsibility for the death, or wondering why the making of so many powerful wishes has not yet drawn the loved one back again. Perhaps being especially good would work the magic? The unnatural calm which goes with this is said to be commoner in girls.

This kind of behaviour can also follow the death of a brother or sister who had been regarded as the family favourite. 'Why wasn't it me?' is rarely spoken out loud. Whatever its cause, a child's quiet withdrawal is less likely to be noticed if someone else, more obviously upset, is attracting all the attention.

Angry aggression

A young man known to me is now in his twenties but well remembers, as a four year old, being left with a family friend in Uganda when his parents, for serious reasons, had to return to England. On their departure, he climbed as high as he could up a tree and stayed there until drawn down by hunger. Even then, he threw his spaghetti supper at the new caregiver and cried for his mother. It is interesting that he is now a carer for people in crisis.

This angry reaction to loss is often commoner in boys. When it is not recognised as the anger of grief, they risk getting into further trouble for 'being so naughty at a time like this'. It rubs salt into the wound to be asked, 'What would your Mummy say?' if her absence is what lies at the root of the trouble. There may already be a sense of uneasy guilt that perhaps she has gone away because of his naughtiness.

Bad behaviour may thus be the child's way of provoking what is seen to be a deserved punishment. Perhaps, once the score is settled, the absent one may return. Reassurance that the child is not to blame brings the sad but slow realisation that the loved one will not be coming back. This can be accompanied by even more angry aggression. It would be all too easy to miss the grief behind it all.

Clinging or regression

Other changes in behaviour are common, including relapse into the behaviour of an earlier level of development. Sleeping or eating upsets are common, sometimes with bedwetting or soiling. There is often a desperate clinging to someone (particularly a sole surviving parent) and strong reluctance to be left alone or to go to school. Once in the classroom, attention may wander. Teachers need to be particularly alert to all these indicators of unresolved grief.

Practical help

Going along with the babyishness for a time is better than trying to brace a child with appeals to 'Be your age'. Plenty of quiet cuddles and the readiness by adults to accept (and sometimes share) sudden tearfulness will all be comforting.

When normal rhythms are upset there are a number of things which may help to restore them. Having small helpings of favourite food, going to bed wrapped in a blanket with a favourite toy, having a nightlight or gentle music in the bedroom, or sleeping near enough to someone who will try to soothe away bad dreams can each be consoling. These little extras, if supplied without undue fuss, can be gently and quietly withdrawn when the child's behaviour returns to normal but this may be a matter of months. It will not be helpful to worry about bedwetting during this time. The child will be upset by it, but can be reassured that it will in time get better again.

Sometimes the child's drawings will give windows into the mind. Watching what the child does in play may also be revealing, especially 'Let's pretend' games. Children love to have stories read to them and there are now a number of little books available which deal with someone's death. All these activities can start up conversation.

This age group will be readier to talk than some

older children would be and can be helped by a teacher or parent who expresses understanding and affection.

Keeping memories alive

Photograph albums and scrapbooks of events in the life of the loved one, even those which happened before the children were born, are always good to have. A 'memory box' could also contain some characteristic garment, such as Daddy's old tweed cap, Mummy's favourite scarf (perhaps still holding a whiff of her perfume), a brother's drawings or a sister's home-made doll. Ideas will be different and special for each family.

Anniversaries can be changed from occasions for sadness to days for recollecting more joyful times, helped perhaps by old family videos or just talking about the funny things the departed one used to say or do. The children are likely to wonder how things are in heaven and whether there will be a heavenly birthday party. Such imaginings are consoling and should not be discouraged. Openness and mutual understanding will help with the ongoing long haul of bereavement, just as they did at its start. As Marc's father said, 'The sharing of the bereavement with the children, however young, and talking to them, helped tremendously. When we had discussed this beforehand, I was bitterly opposed to it, but I must say, having seen the results, I would strongly recommend it.'

Points to remember for children of about 3–7 years old:

*Fact and fancy can be hard to disentangle.
*Descriptions need to match experience if they are to have much meaning.
*Viewing the body and attending the funeral do not hold the impact felt by adults: many children still believe that death is reversible.
*It is comforting to be included in a family occasion even when it is a sad one.
*Changed behaviour or new symptoms can indicate grief.

Helpful Bible passages:

2 Corinthians 5:1–9
Lamentations 3:22–24; 31–33
Psalm 119:76

Further reading:

Daphne Batty (ed.), HIV *infection and children in need* (London, British Association of Adoption and Fostering 1993).

Marilyn and Graham Cotton, with Janet Goodall, '*A brother dies at home*', *Maternal and Child Health, vol* 6, No 7, (1981) pp.288–292.

Rosemary Wells, *Helping children cope with grief* (London, Sheldon Press 1988).

For children:

Jan Godfrey, *The Cherry Blossom Tree* (London,

Tamarind 1996)
Susan Varley, *Badger's parting gifts* (London, Picture Lions, HarperCollins 1992).
Susan Varley, *Badger's parting gifts* (London, Picture Lions, HarperCollins 1992).

7

Sudden death: helping 3–7 year olds

A three year old can have a lovely sense of 'My wish is their command,' especially when stage-managing a temper tantrum in the supermarket. The bigger the gallery, the less likely are parents to walk out and leave the performance. The child's face-value judgment suggests that wishes can often be fulfilled simply by wishing (or digging in the heels) hard enough.

At an age where logical deduction still lies ahead, which includes early primary school years, some wish fulfilments must seem quite magical. Yet they can be frightening, too.

Wish fulfilment or disaster?

The three year old brother of a new baby may think that she is stealing his own previously well-managed show. He can accordingly wish her back to where she came from. If she then vanishes, the effect on his parents can seem to him like a nightmare, not a dream fulfilled. A child's mistaken sense of being responsible for such family disasters can go on into early school years.

A little girl of five or six, who had longed for a baby brother, was thrilled when her parents produced one although, unknown to her, he had inoperable spina bifida. A few weeks later, she was reported to have 'gone off the baby' and was spending a lot of time playing alone in the garden. This sounded unusual for the big sister of a young baby, but it transpired that, not wanting to upset her, the parents had not told her about the baby's problems. After discussion, they decided to show her his poorly back at bath time and explain how sad they were that no-one could put this right, though he still needed to be loved. The child had a good cry, but then came back to sharing in his care again. His eventual death was not the sudden shock to her that it could have been.

Grief overlooked can cause trouble later

To have suffered an important loss under the age of seven years is one of the life events often described by people who suffer later on from chronic depression. These adults of today are unlikely to have met with the attuned understanding which we are now learning to offer in bereavement at any age. If we are to reduce lifelong emotional scars in today's children, we need to stay tuned. If left undealt with, the feelings aroused

by their early hurts can lie hidden but smouldering on. They may continue to disrupt emotional life for years.

This was true for a six year old who suddenly lost his father. This was not through death, as the man walked away from his family, then never made contact again. Six years later his son was brought to see me because of behaviour problems which had caused trouble ever since.

I asked the boy whether he could remember when his Dad had left and he immediately answered, 'Oh, yes. He was there at breakfast time and he said, "Goodbye, I'll see you after work," but he never did come back.'

'Why do you think he went away like that?' I asked. Without hesitation, as though he had gone over the scene many times in his mind, he replied, 'I thought it was because me and my sister Karen had been quarrelling.' In the disruption of home life at the time, his own needs had not been dealt with, so had continued to be acted out for years.

To step into the shoes of such children can help us to recognise the confusion within. Feelings of power, guilt, rejection and loss can each add to a hurt child's bewilderment. A blade may have fallen suddenly and sharply, slicing in on normal life or cutting out someone's life altogether, and it can seem to each one (still tending to be 'me-centred') that he or she has been the one to provoke it. Whatever is going to happen next? Anxious dispositions may have their beginnings here.

Death comes suddenly

A sudden death gives no time for careful preparation. The car careers off the road, the gunman comes to the door, the heart attack strikes or one day the baby does not wake up and all these families are plunged into acute grief. Amongst many of them will be young children who, in the crisis, are quite likely to be taken out of the way.

This could immediately say to them that they are being held responsible for what is going on and are no longer wanted. They may not have been told what has happened, though many have had one brief, terrifying glimpse. Even when adults offer explanations they can be very bewildering and a basis for fearful fantasies.

Andrew was three years old and went with his mother to wake up his baby brother. He screamed as he saw her scoop up the baby with blood coming from his nose and then run out to the telephone box. Andrew was later left with a neighbour. He did not see the baby again.

A few days later, he was taken to a family party. In fact, this was just after the funeral service, though he was told that the party was being given for him. Later he was taken to the cemetery and shown the flowers on a grave which his parents said was where the baby was now. As they had also told him that the baby was with Jesus he asked how he could be in two places at once, but got no satisfactory answer. After all this, he became very frightened about nosebleeds and asked if he, too, would die if he had one. He was still very upset a month later. If he saw his mother crying he tried to comfort her by saying that when they went on their next holiday the baby would be there waiting for them.

He would still have been sad to have shared the truth, but to be left in such bewilderment was also very upsetting.

Trying to get it right

It is painful, but in the end easier, to handle things properly in the first place than it is to try and put right what has already gone so wrong. Little children do know, even from poking at dead moths or flies, or seeing someone's catch of fish, that what once was alive can die, no longer breathing, moving or responding.

By three years old, most children know about death and by five can grasp that it involves not being able to move any more and so means being separated from everyone else. The idea that dead bodies cannot eat, breathe or respond and dead people do not come back is clear to most (but not all) children by the age of six.

These are the answers children would probably give if asked their ideas about death, but it seems likely that they would absorb more, even when younger, by seeing, touching and observing for themselves. Even so, for those who have missed out on that kind of involvement, it should be possible to match up the idea that, just as an insect or fish lies still after death, so the one who has gone was dead and still, too. Such explanations would help if a young child had not been able to see the dead body.

Unbelievers may stop there, although even their children, still not used to thinking in abstract terms, may copy adults and speak of heaven as the dead person's new whereabouts. Equally, in life they might have talked of someone's going to Spain. By now, in the child's eyes, if you have gone, you must have gone somewhere. Heaven can accordingly be a useful word to know even if for many it is empty of meaning.

Young children can be very matter of fact. Tim, aged three, lost his ten month old brother by death round about the same time as the family's pet fish had died and been sent to a watery grave. His bedtime prayer was arresting. 'Dear God, please bless Robert up in heaven and our goldfish who's gone down the lavatory.'

A Christian family, despite their grief, can speak confidently of a real hope which goes beyond death. Even though the idea of heaven may not be understood very well, it must be a good place to be if it is the home of the Lord Jesus, whose name is already so dear and special.

Stillbirth, neonatal death and 'cot' death

The sudden, unexpected death of an infant, either before or after birth, can remain a mystery to adults. The death of a baby who was born too soon or too small to survive is easier to explain. When an extremely preterm baby miscarries, how much other children are to be involved will depend on how long and how eagerly they had been anticipating the new arrival.

The sudden death of an infant already known and loved is one of the most shattering of losses. The only honest thing to say to young children then is, 'We don't know why it happens, but it only happens to babies, not to big children like you. In any case, it doesn't happen very often. But we are very sad that it happened to our baby. Would you like to come with us to say goodbye?'

In all these circumstances, seeing for themselves the lifelessness of a dead baby, even one whom they had only hoped to know, will help little children more than a lot of words. Being supported in saying goodbye in person helps to bring understanding. (See also pages 53, 82.)

If, however, seeing the body or joining in the farewells has not been encouraged (and it is very understandable that in their own sudden shock and grief parents do not know what to do for the best) it may help bewildered little ones for a parent or other familiar grown-up to sit down with them, apologise that in the upset things had not been explained properly before and then to say plainly that the infant is dead. This would itself be an end to the mystery and could bring some relief rather than immediate grief. It would also help for someone to go through the story of the baby's birth, or how the body was found, explaining how it was clear that the child really was dead. If the funeral is already over, that should also be described.

It could help some children to go through what they thought had happened by using a small doll, which is so obviously different from a living baby in its total lack of responsiveness. Putting it away in a box could be a way of acting out disposal of the coffin. If seen playing this through again, this should be understood as a child's way of absorbing facts, not merely as ghoulish interest.

When it is clear that the atmosphere holds not a breath of blame towards them, bereft young children will be helped to experience the reality of death without feeling somehow to blame.

Trying to explain modes of sudden death

In so many parts of the world, accidental or violent death is common. Whether or not this was witnessed by a victim's children, it still needs to be spelled out to them how such a tragedy happened. They will need to be assured that they are not responsible and could not have prevented it. Again, truth sometimes needs to be unfolded in stages so that one fact is absorbed at a time.

News that the person is dead will itself be hard enough to take in. The short explanation, 'She was killed in an accident,' will mean more to an adult than to a child, who is so often excused for some act of clumsiness with, 'We know it was an accident.' The information may be dutifully received, but without the truth sinking in. Trying to explain how the death came about can thus be quite difficult.

Violent death

After a road accident, for example, the ambulance team sometimes manages to keep the victim alive long enough to get on to a life-support machine in an intensive care unit. This gives a little more time for the family to register what is happening and to think of the needs of the children. There is an understandable reluctance to let them see for themselves what may be serious physical damage, but explanations without experience are hard to take in.

If someone has been badly hurt and is disfigured or heavily bandaged, it is best to describe this first and, even better, to go through the most striking features with the help of a crayon drawing. Some units provide a doll (or could be lent one) on which an artist's impression can be made or bandages applied, helping to prepare children for what they will see. Unless they themselves say that they want to go no further, someone familiar should then go with them.

The reality is usually much less scary to a child than it would be for most adults entering an intensive care unit. At least it shows that things are being done which could not be done at home. To the child, the reunion spells lack of blame and this bonus of a brief time together can make all the difference between total confusion and better understanding.

Death by suicide

Rates of suicide are increasing rapidly all over the

world. In many so-called developed countries, the highest rates are in young people in their mid-teens to twenties. So great is the shock, grief and often guilt amongst senior members of a family when this happens that it can become a dark, unmentioned secret. It may therefore never be explained to the younger ones at all, even if they had found the body or seen the police come to the house.

Yet hushing it all up at home will not stop rumours reaching school. A child would be even more hurt by being told such news crassly by another child than to have the news broken gently by someone close and trustworthy.

The favoured method of suicide for British men is to inhale fumes from the exhaust of a car, or to hang themselves. For women it is to take poison or drugs. These methods leave features undamaged, though possibly discoloured or distorted. In America and Australia, suicide by shotgun is commoner, so is often damaging to the face. Funeral directors can be very skilful and, for anyone who saw the body just after the deed was done, it could leave better memories to look again when they have done their sensitive work.

Having to break the news of a death is awful anyway, but how to break the news of a self-inflicted death to a child can be one of the hardest dilemmas of all. It will usually be a parent or older brother or sister whose behaviour has to be explained. A period of depression beforehand may already have made young children feel that they must have done something wrong. For Daddy to have become so remote and now to have decided to go altogether must surely mean that he had stopped loving them. After someone's suicide, guilt is common to the rest of the family, children included. They need to have it made clear that the death was not their fault.

Explanations should include mention of how ill the person was. 'Even though he looked just the same outside, Daddy's mind must have been very tired and sad inside. You can tell how he wasn't thinking straight by what he decided to do.'

A clear statement as to what method was used should not, for this age, be dressed up. The full horror will be more likely to register in older age groups, when clearer insight has developed. Until then, the child will feel sorry but is not yet likely to identify in depth with the mental and physical pain involved in such an act.

As this experience is not confined to unbelieving families, it is also comforting to know that, even though it was a terrible thing to do, the one who has died will be taken care of by the Lord Jesus and is free from all those unhappy feelings. Should the obvious question come, 'Why didn't Jesus stop Daddy doing it?' the only honest answer is, 'I don't know. Perhaps he did try to tell him not to, but Daddy was too poorly to listen.'

What if no-one is allowed to see?

When the death has been sudden or violent, the police will have had the body removed. In a few cases, the damage may be disfiguring enough for the coroner to recommend that no-one should see what has happened. To help a child then, this would mean thinking up a matching description. 'What do you think would happen to people sitting in one of your toy cars if another car crashed into them?' or, 'You've seen fighting on the TV news, and how the guns go bang and sometimes people get killed. This is what happened to Uncle John.'

It will be difficult, though, for children to try and imagine someone known and loved being in such a situation. It may help them to go and say goodbye to a photograph, perhaps with someone who can indicate the site of the injuries, or to spend some quiet moments on the loved one's bed cuddling a familiar garment. It can be openly shared with the child how sad everyone feels not to have been able to say these farewells in person. Shared tears can bring comforting closeness.

Chapels of rest

Even serious injuries can be bandaged up and autopsy scars concealed. Visiting a chapel of rest can be very reassuring, even after a violent death. Our own kindly neighbourhood funeral director told me how children (and adults, too) can be relieved by a reality less awful than either their imagination or overheard remarks had led them to expect. I was also told that a major problem was often caused by grandparents who misguidedly tried to prevent the children's admission. A grandparent can often be a child's best friend, but when trying to spare children pain events must always be looked at from a child's viewpoint. The effects of both cautious officialdom and family prejudice could give children more nightmares than facing the truth would have done.

In practice, at the chapel of rest off a mortuary, a Moses basket is normally used for babies, otherwise the body lies on a wide bier of fixed height. Except for the head and face, everything else is usually concealed by a rather regal cover of purple velvet. The effect is solemn and rather distant, but no-one need feel rushed and I have found the attendants to be kind and understanding.

The funeral director's chapel of rest is likely to be smaller and so a little more personal. Although lying in a coffin, the body looks very natural and is usually dressed in familiar clothes. In my experience, the height of this bier is adjustable. Small viewers will see better if the coffin can be brought down closer to their level and are unlikely to be upset by what they see. Again, lingering is allowed and the atmosphere is entirely sympathetic.

Guilt and grace

Children are helped greatly to be assured that a death was not their fault. Their sense of loss will be as great as that following other sudden deaths, but if it comes as an abrupt end to a depressive or other protracted illness, there can also be a sense of a cloud having lifted. Guilty relief then also needs to be owned. Previous unkind thoughts or words or deeds may come back, not only to the child perhaps, including earlier wishes that Daddy would either start to be nice again or go away. The little boy described at the beginning of this chapter could have felt like this after his baby sister's death.

Guilt can be met by grace. It would help each member of a Christian family, little ones included, to confess the times when they had had nasty thoughts and then to ask to be forgiven. Older ones may later have to forgive themselves, too. The relief of some young children after such a prayer to the Lord Jesus and their evident trust that he has forgiven them can be a telling reminder of God's grace to everyone else.

The funeral and afterwards

Sudden, unexpected death has to be followed by an inquest and sometimes it takes many weeks before the funeral can be held. The advantage of the delay is that between the death, inquest and funeral, the initially shocked adults have had time to move from a position of denying access to the children to one which understands and includes them. It is good that this is becoming much more usual at all family funerals.

I was once at the thanksgiving service for an old friend whose grandchildren were also present. They were solemn, attentive and composed. In my mind's eye, I could see in his old garden a little row of memorials which marked the graves of 'Hattie's babies' (who were rabbits) and 'Gerbie Howard' (the gerbil). Children who have been encouraged to hold funerals for their dead pets have at the same time been prepared for family funerals. They will know that the loved one's body is in the coffin. This time, they will have been told, the coffin is to be brought into church for a special farewell to the person who has died and a special thankyou to God that he or she had ever lived. The coffin and the body inside it will then be put right away as they are now no use to anyone.

From about three years old upwards, children may more readily grasp the purpose of a funeral service. Those likely to be very restless should be helped to see that this could make other people more unhappy, so someone (not a chief mourner) would then need to take them outside. If given a careful account of what is to happen, though, even quite small children can become very absorbed in watching how everything is done.

If young children come both to the service and to any tea party which follows, death will not then be seen as a cause only for solemnity or only for celebration. At both gatherings, the presence of children is a reminder to their elders that life goes on and there are still others left to live for.

Explaining burial and cremation

However well prepared they are for the purpose of the service, young children can find very confusing the conflicting ideas of someone's being with Jesus in heaven but at the same time going to be buried in the ground or burnt up. Not until an average child is about eight years old will a dead body be understood not only to be unresponsive but also unable to feel discomfort. As with Christopher in chapter 3, a matching idea will be a help.

Anything which may be familiar to a child which in nature leaves an empty shell (as a snail does) or an empty cell (as a wasp or bee does) or which changes from one form to another (as a chick from an eggshell, a frog from a tadpole or a butterfly from a chrysalis all do) would provide a helpful comparison. Even a young town-dweller could find a snailshell, see empty eggshells in the nesting box or be taken to a grocer who stocked honey in the comb. For some, an illustrated natural history book may have to suffice.

Trying to imagine something not yet seen can be hard, but to hold an empty shell in the hand is to see how clearly the imagery fits. (If breakfast eggshells are used, it must be made clear what would have happened if the eggs had been left with the hen!) To show a child the chick's old home, now empty and useless, matches well with the obvious emptiness of a lifeless body.

The one to have moved out has finished with the old shelter for ever, so it can safely be disposed of. There is no fear of the chick, for example, being trapped inside whilst its old shell is being buried or burnt up. It is something like that when someone we love has died. We of course feel very sad to be left behind, but it must be lovely for the one who has gone away to be with the Lord Jesus. One day, when he comes back again himself, he will give new bodies to us all, including the people who trusted him when they died, but until then we will not see them again.

The pangs which so assail older hearts as death slices into a family are unknown to very much younger ones. The inner acceptance that separation during our earthly life is final may not yet come home to them for years. This can make them try to relieve adult grief by talking about their hopes of reunion. This can be hard to take, but repeating the painful truth helps everyone involved to come slowly to terms with the reality of the loss. This is the first difficult but essential task to be faced in all bereavements.

Life goes on

Some parents find solace in visiting the cemetery and can assume that children will find this helpful as well. This may not be so. Until they can read the names on a headstone or realise what it means to have buried a body, there are better places where it could be helpful for young children to go and remember the one who has gone. To sit on his chair and think how Daddy used to sit there, or to look in their own garden at growing things which Mummy helped them to plant, could be helpful to bereft children and also to their adult companions.

Old photographs can stir memories of happier days. It will also help to think of the dear one enjoying a new life in the trusted company of the Lord Jesus. 'We don't know whether Daddy can still see us, but we do still love each other.'

Young relatives often quickly commandeer a

dead child's toys, or ask for his tracksuit, or her old bedroom. This often seems to adults to be grasping or greedy, or to be happening too soon, yet it is only a child's way of holding on to precious memories and valued mementos when so much else has changed.

Recognising children's grief (See also page 86)

The shock of a sudden death probably brings the most overwhelming grief of all. To remember that the children will be grieving, too, is the first step towards looking for the evidence.

As all concerned will be shocked and bewildered, seeking professional advice early on could help everyone's grief, including the child's, to start to resolve normally. This is particularly important when a child of any age witnesses some form of sudden, unexpected death.

Young children do not spell out their feelings to anybody, even if they could find the words to do so. Yet for their first seven years or so they are likely to feel somehow responsible for a family disaster and think that everyone is blaming them. Each is probably scared both by the event and what may follow.

Some may adopt a protective covering of unnatural goodness and quietness, which can be misread as being very thoughtful and considerate. Alternatively, behaviour may suddenly change for the worse. Many children endure a time of great bewilderment and a sense of alienation whilst the grown-ups either overlook their needs or argue about what to say to them.

Teachers can be a great help, both to the child in person and in helping other children to understand their friend's need.

It helps to be included

Perhaps the greatest help of all to children who grieve after a sudden death will be for someone to tell them, however painfully, what has to be told and then to include them in what has to be done. They are then able to feel the strength of adult sympathy and sadness, knowing themselves at last to be allowed to share in it. Tears may flow, but they are no longer the bitter tears of children who feel isolated and unwanted. (See also page 89.)

At such times, a small child's bedtime prayers can go straight to the point, reminding older members of the family that the person now being missed so much can be lovingly entrusted to the care of the one who has promised, in the end, to wipe away all our tears.

Points to remember for children about 3–7 years old:

*Children of this age are used to being upset.
*They are also used to being made to feel guilty.
*Understanding depends on experience: seeing is believing.
*Grief is not always obvious.
*Changed behaviour can spell confusion and sadness.

*It hurts more to feel excluded than to be sad together.

Helpful Bible passages:
Psalm 42
Psalm 46:1–3
1 Corinthians 15:51–57
Revelation 21:3, 4

Further reading:

Phyllis Kilbourne (ed.), *Healing the children of war: a handbook for ministry to children who have suffered deep traumas* (California, MARC Publications, World Vision International 1995).

Richard Lansdown, 'Communicating with children' in Ann Goldman (ed.), *Care of the dying child* (Oxford, Oxford University Press 1994).

Barbara Ward et al, *Good grief 1 and 2; Exploring feelings, loss and death with under elevens* 2nd. edn. (London, Jessica Kingsley Publishers 1993).

For children:

Freddie McKeowen, *Which came first? A book of life-cycles* (London, Medici Society Ltd 1990).

8

The dying child: helping 3–7 year olds

When watching televised debates or even towards the end of a rather wearisome committee meeting, it can add a new (though naughty) dimension to try to tune in to the mental ages being assumed by the participants, as judged by their methods of reasoning. 'Me, here, now' still features sometimes, as does putting together disconnected items, or making one thing mean another. Deductive reasoning can be spoiled by face value judgment or fantasy and what one person thinks has been safely disposed of can be resurrected by another. Some do not seem to look very far ahead or recognise the implications of what is going on. In other words, the outlook can be very much like that of children in this three to seven age group.

I am giving more space to these children than to others simply because they can have the most problems both in clarifying their own ideas and being understood by those who want to help them.

Sudden death

All over the world, accidents and overwhelming infections are the major causes of death amongst young children.

Sudden life-threatening illness

When such an illness arises, there may be no time at all for the child to feel more than tired or sick before unconsciousness intervenes. Other children may for a short time perceive the vigorous attempts being made to save their lives as personal attacks on them. Depending on personality and previous experience, for a parent to stay alongside during such procedures can be interpreted by the child either as a great comfort or a great collusion with the enemy. A brief explanation may be all that there is time for and not all medical staff encourage parents to join them. Yet it can make all the difference to a child's feelings to hear someone familiar say, 'It will soon be over and then you can have a cuddle. Meantime, hold on to my hand.' Even if the battle for life is eventually lost, it helps to think that the child died supported.

Accidental death

Most children who die suddenly do so after a road accident. If they reach hospital alive, they often go straight to an intensive care unit and are likely to be given artificial respiration on a ventilator. Death usually takes place whilst on the machine, so that it can be hard for the watching relatives to register what is going on or even to stay with the child all the time. The whole experience is a shattering one.

A circle of praying friends can be an immense support. Although surprising recoveries have been known in answer to prayer, even when all has seemed lost, for many families there comes a time when it must be faced that the child cannot be brought back and prayers should now reflect this, asking for comfort rather than cure.

In their disbelief that this is really happening, it can be hard for a family to think of ways to help the one who is about to leave them. In a state of unconsciousness, hearing is probably the last sense to go. This means that it is still worthwhile speaking or singing to (as well as praying with) the dying child, as a known and loved voice may still register and be a comfort.

Four year old Benjy had always loved his mother to sing, 'You are my sunshine'. As he lay unconscious on a ventilator after receiving a serious head injury, she sang it to him again and noticed from the monitor how his heart rate increased. Afterwards, it was a comfort to her to think that perhaps Benjy had felt her continuing presence almost to the end.

Several times in my experience very young children, not necessarily from Christian homes, have indicated a security of spirit, or spoken of seeing someone whose presence was evidently comforting, even when life itself was being threatened. Only a few days before his accident, Benjy had asked his mother whether Jesus would take care of him when he went to sleep and had been happy to be assured that this would be so.

An old lady once wrote to tell me how, as a little girl, she was trapped in a sand tunnel whilst her older brother ran to get help. She had been comforted by a figure in white who sat with her until she was rescued, then disappeared. Another four year old whom I looked after was admitted to hospital with meningitis from which he later died. Twice, before lapsing into coma, he indicated that he could see a presence which, when asked, he said was Jesus.

I am reminded by these episodes of our Lord's love for little children and how he spoke of their angels, evidently ever ready to do the Father's bidding, and how he himself longed to receive them. We can be comforted that he evidently has ways of giving them spiritual companionship when earthly dear ones have to be left behind.

Death comes more slowly

Childhood cancers become commoner at this age and problems present from birth can continue to take their toll.

How young children regard illness

Both the illness and its treatment are likely to be viewed differently by the very young, depending on whether they suddenly intrude or have instead become a familiar part of life.

An otherwise healthy three year old, admitted for a circumcision, told me three years later how he had been held down, kicking and fighting, with a 'gasmask' held firmly over his face. Previously dry at night, he had wet his bed ever since. When I asked, 'Why did you think they were doing that to you?' he said, 'I thought I was being punished for tipping the baby out of his pram.' After his mother and I had explained what had really been happening, the bed-wetting stopped.

Perhaps a seriously ill child endures more passively, but can still be bemused. Yet childhood is a time for receiving many unexpected hurts. Even after uncomfortable tests or treatment, children can be very forgiving, especially if those responsible explain what they are doing and say 'Sorry'.

When there is a little more time, even though the illness is likely to be fatal within days or weeks, parents and hospital staff need to work out between them the best way of explaining treatment to a child of up to about seven years old. This will naturally depend on the nature of the illness.

Explaining treatment to a child

Many children under seven think that being ill is their own fault, so many must also see their treatment in the same light. Perhaps the most important thing to convey to all young patients is that, however uncomfortable it may be, treatment is not a punishment, but is trying to make them well again. (The word 'better' is likely to slip out, but could indicate to some children that, after all, they had been bad.) To get this across, a grown-up who is close to the child will have to try to get back into a young skin again.

From three years old onwards, *an appeal to age* often seems to inspire little children to cooperate. This is not to repeat the old untruth about big boys not crying but saying instead, 'What a good thing you're three and not two any more because you're big enough now to help us by holding very still.' A remark like this needs to be slipped in before the lips start to tremble as this is also the age for a very negative reaction to unwelcome attention.

A very *simple explanation*, couched in familiar terms, is best given *immediately before* a procedure. If information is given too far ahead it may not be connected to the event. 'There's going to be a little pinprick, then that's it,' gives clear enough warning. Then, at the crucial moment, the child's *inability to pay close attention to two things at once* is a useful ally. A *distraction*, such as, 'Squeeze my fingers as hard as you can,' may mean that the episode is over before it has really registered.

Attempts to distract a child's attention become more transparent as the ability develops to make connections and so to recognise what is likely to be upsetting. The appearance of the 'pricker lady' at the bedside and the skill with which she does or does not take blood samples will soon be matched up, producing faith or fear as the learned response.

During a test which is tedious rather than painful, *diversion*, for example by story telling, can bring calm by taking away attention from other immediate problems.

If medicine can be taken by mouth, it may be helped to go down with the spoonful of sugar so tunefully recommended by Mary Poppins, or (better for the teeth during a long illness) after sucking an ice chip to freeze the taste buds. When drugs are used to relieve terminal symptoms, their use should be explained as the child can now observe how helpful they usually are.

All this is designed to minimise the pain of the descent, although some discomfort may remain. However, the child who has arrived at death's door often takes therapy so quietly and patiently that onlookers can be very moved and strengthened themselves. Towards the end, a state of increasing drowsiness usually supervenes, gently pulling a curtain across acute awareness of what is going on. It must provide a last comfort to hear familiar voices and to feel familiar arms whose clasp is only loosened as the child goes to be 'safe in the arms of Jesus'.

The experience of long, life-threatening illness

For some children, the illness may have begun in babyhood and they have grown up with it. Given normal intelligence, they may then show a degree of understanding which is ahead of the average for their chronological age. Just as adults may be said to have aged after going through hard times, so older heads can be put onto young shoulders by experiences not usual for their age group. This will need to be gauged when making approaches to individual children.

Feeling different from others

A little girl with a congenitally shortened arm and leg realised, on starting primary school at five years old, that not only did other children have limbs of equal length, which she had noticed before, but that this meant that she was the one to be unusual, which was a new idea to her. Her mind had grown up from the 'me-centred' state of infancy and was now at the next stage of matching and classifying. She was, she could now see, in a class of her own.

Such growth in understanding could also come to a child with a life-threatening illness who has to miss playgroup or school for hospital treatment and starts to realise that this is not so for anyone else. Gradually more complex differences are recognised such as, 'I bruise a lot', 'I have lots of doctors', 'My hair has fallen out so I wear a wig'. Until this understanding arrives, even a major difference may be accepted as a fact of life both by the child and by playmates. They have not yet arrived at the age for making accurate deductions.

Other children at this stage do not yet understand what is implied when a friend can no longer keep up, or is often absent due to illness. This again is providential protection, saving the sick child from the added pain of being treated as a misfit.

Serious differences between a sick child and others are likely to be clearer to them all by six or seven years old. Again there is a built-in protection as this is also when other children are beginning to reach out sympathetically to anyone in trouble, such as a school friend who is unwell. There are children, of course, who can be unkind to anyone, but one who has a genuine illness is less likely to be teased or bullied than others who may be regarded as weaklings.

Exclusion from school

When going to school becomes too much, being kept at home may not be linked by the child with the illness but instead be seen as having been expelled from school in disgrace, particularly if it comes after some minor disagreement there. Parents need to tune in to this possible way of looking at things and remind the child of their previous explanations about the illness.

Particularly when everyone knows that the child is likely to die soon, messages tend to drop off and the child can feel abandoned by old friends. I have sometimes had to telephone a past teacher to point this out. Not feeling free to say 'Get well soon' does not mean that there is nothing more to be said. It can cheer the sick child so much to have messages or pictures sent home by old schoolmates and it can be even better, when not too ill, to have short visits from a few special friends.

Explanations may need to be updated

A child who has had a disability for years will grow in maturity of outlook as time goes on. Explanations given to a three year old will therefore need to be revised as understanding increases. A six to seven year old's sudden refusal to accept treatment which was previously taken like a lamb may simply be an indication that the child does not see the need for it, so this will have to be explained. (See also page 148.)

Although names for the external parts of the body are by now well known, its internal arrangements still cannot be seen in the mind's eye. The tapping of the heart, beating behind the chest wall, can easily be felt and so can the movement of the chest on taking a big breath. The child may obediently repeat 'heart' and 'lungs' as the given explanation for these observations, yet without quite understanding what they have to do with feeling breathless. Explanations are probably still best expressed in matching terms. 'Before you had this medicine, you couldn't even run as far as the gate to meet Daddy without getting puffed,' or, 'If we stop these antibiotics, your nasty cough will come back.'

For the child with a chronic chest illness or a malignant disease, it may be an acceptable idea to talk of a fight going on inside the body. 'Your defenders need help from your treatment so that they can overcome the invaders. When the defenders start to win, you should start to feel stronger again.'

Naming the disease

It is not a bad idea to establish familiarity with the name of a disease before any deeper insight develops. Caregivers may prefer to speak plainly of cancer cells being like the invaders and this phrase will be repeated without knowing either what 'cancer' or 'cells' actually mean.

Parents may hesitate to use this kind of language, but the confident use of adult phrases does not yet mean adult understanding. If there are older children in the family, though, time to explain more fully will need to be given to them, with the initial reassurance that most forms of childhood cancer, as well as other illnesses, usually respond well to the start of treatment.

One possible exception to naming the illness may be HIV infection or AIDS. Here, it may be better simply to talk about an infection of the blood. This would be to protect the child from being avoided by other people, not from the knowledge itself. The pros and cons of handling this may clarify as this spectrum of disease becomes better understood by everyone. As with cancer, it could be a better state of affairs for a child to grow up knowing the truth, even without at first wholly understanding it, but each family will need to think about this in the light of their own context.

It may be a relief to stop active treatment

Going to and from hospital, first feeling ill and then better again, can gradually become the normal lifestyle. It may therefore take time for it to dawn on everyone, especially the child, that there is now to be no more getting well again.

It may eventually be a relief rather than a concern that some unpleasant forms of treatment are then stopped, although it can be a greater worry to the child that those near and dear seem to have become tenser and sadder. Again, it could be a reassurance rather than a shock to be told, 'We aren't upset with you but with the invaders. They seem to be winning, but the good thing is that you won't need to go to hospital so often and we can all be together more.'

Stopping futile treatment is not the same as giving up. Other drugs aimed at comfort, given round the clock, will ease pain. Finding distractions along all the five senses of sight, sound, touch, taste and smell is something with which brothers and sisters could help, as well as thinking up other gentle games and diversions. To tell or read stories to the dying child, especially the old, old story of Jesus and his love, can be very comforting. Inner peace can be experienced, and sometimes understood, as his healing touch, even when there is now no hope of physical cure. This can be a time of special togetherness for a family, particularly when their trust is in him.

'Am I going to die?'

It may come as a surprise to pose a question like this here, after all that we have been saying about the mindset of this age group being one which does not usually range very far ahead.

It is important to remember that a child whose experience has been wider than most is likely to have been matured by it. This includes those who have suffered long and difficult illnesses and sometimes distressing treatment. Not only do certain symptoms become matched with certain consequences, but gradually the child develops sufficient know-how to anticipate the next step. A naturally bright child will also be quicker to grasp the truth about what is happening.

When attending the same specialist clinic, the news of another child's death could also bring a clearer realisation that the same fate could be looming, especially for a child of the same age. Yet although the fact of death may be understood by now, this does not apply to the way in which it usually happens (except as portrayed on the media). It is surprising what a child can tolerate without any obvious worry about what will happen next. The Creator's kind design helps to protect the very young from insights which can be so painful to their elders.

Marc was found to have a lump in his tummy before he was two years old and immediately had a kidney removed because of a malignant tumour. For the next four years he endured cycles of therapy which made him bald, radiotherapy which made him sick, periods of remission when life was normal, whooping cough when he nearly died, two more operations and finally such widespread disease as to make him blind in one eye and paralysed below the waist. Throughout he made no comment on his sufferings other than to cry if in severe discomfort. Between relapses, he had a full and happy life at home and at school. He once surprised me by letting loose a snail called Sammy on to my hospital outpatient desk. He was a very lively, lovable and loving little boy.

When the blind eye and the paralysis developed it was clear that there was now no hope of curing Marc. He was given morphine to relieve his pain, other drugs to stop his vomiting and treatment for his recurrent nosebleeds. All this therapy was regularly adjusted so that he remained alert enough to enjoy drawing, painting and playing with his sisters. He never asked why he could no longer see so well or use his legs. His mother later said, 'Although he couldn't move from the waist downwards he was very cheerful from the waist upwards.'

It was at this stage that his sisters, aged four and nine years old, were warned about the seriousness of his illness. Yet how much did he understand and how much should he be told about what lay ahead? Marc had a friend called David, who had leukaemia and attended the same hospital for similar treatment. The two families also went to the same church. After repeated cycles of treatment, David grew worse and died. Not long afterwards, when still only five and a half years old, Marc suddenly asked his mother, 'Mum, is it going to happen to me like it happened to David?'

None of us could blame his mother for her immediately protective answer, 'Don't be so silly, of course not.' In telling about this later she added, 'But I felt that I'd let him down by not telling him the truth. We had always told him the truth.'

One good delaying tactic would have been for her to ask him to say more clearly what he meant. He could have been asking if his nose was going to bleed as David's had done, or whether he, too, was never going to go back to school. Clarifying the question might have helped with the answer, but very understandably his mother feared the worst and temporarily closed the door to further discussion.

A fifteen year old would have seen the pain and panic in his mother's face and asked someone else next time. Marc was not yet able to enter deeply into another person's feelings, or to realise how difficult a question he had posed, but he still wanted to know the answer. It was not long before he asked his question again, quite directly: 'Am I going to die, Mum?'

His mother reported later, 'When he said it, I wished the world would swallow me up and I didn't have to answer. I just said to him that he was very, very poorly and that we all had to die sometime, but that he wasn't going to die that day. He accepted this and afterwards we felt that it was the most truthful thing that we had said to him.' There had been no need to bring in any talk of heaven, or moving house. He was happy enough to live from day to day, at home with his family, without any more ever being said to him about his death.

Answering 'not today' to an older child might have brought the rejoinder, 'Well, when will it be?' At five years old, such elasticity of mind had not yet arrived and Marc was content with the answer given. His mother had managed to be honest and comforting at the same time. He knew that the worst part of his treatment had stopped and was quite content simply to be at home.

His parents were forewarned of his likely mode of death, which would be for him to become weaker and sleepier, and after a month at home this is just what happened. He had been chatting to his parents within hours of his death and they were both with him as he died. His closest ties held firm to the end.

Recognising and helping the dying child's sadness

The great protection from sadness, particularly at the younger end of this age group, is that most of these children do not usually worry too much about what will happen next, except in the short term. An exception would be if something perplexing had been overheard.

Sometimes, worry is picked up from anxious tension within the family, part of which may come from the parents' concern over whether to speak and what to say if the dying child asks any questions. These, if they surface, are most likely to be asked of someone in the family rather than anyone outside it, such as a teacher or nurse. However, not all children can find the right words and, because they may not yet be able to look at things from someone else's viewpoint, can also assume that everyone else has the same thoughts but is keeping them quiet.

It is worth any caregiver thinking of this tension should new symptoms develop. These may not always indicate that the disease is advancing, but could be due to secret anxiety. Such symptoms may include withdrawal from previously enjoyed activities, or unusual tummyache or headache. Sleeplessness or bedwetting could also be clues to an emotional rather than a physical cause. It may be hard to help the child to unburden for the same reason as the anxiety has arisen; the right words are hard to find.

Bad dreams are as yet not always recognised as being mere dreams but if reported may give the adults a window into the child's mind. A little child at play may act out the problem and an older child may draw revealing pictures. Both these activities, if viewed sympathetically and imaginatively, could lead to helpful conversation. This would offer an easier opening for the child than a direct question such as, 'Is anything worrying you?' as it could be even more worrying then not to know what to say.

Not all children need or want to discuss their condition in great depth. This was true for a little boy who was dying and whose parents asked me to 'talk to him about it', as they felt unable to face doing this themselves, yet thought that he could be worrying. I discovered that he liked trains. The highlight of his young life, in fact, had been going on a train to Crewe. He could not do that now as he was so poorly.

I mentioned fairly casually that sometimes, when people are ill, they wonder if they will ever get well again and even if they are going to die. The look he gave me agreed, so I went on to say that death was not something to be afraid of. In some ways, it was a little bit like his trip to Crewe. You go on a journey to a place you've really wanted to go to and it's lovely when you get there.

It was tempting for me to push the application further, but he made it clear that he'd had enough for one day. It was also enough to ease the tension, both for him and for his parents. The subject of death had been mentioned without trying to cover it up, yet also without at once applying it to his own condition. It could safely be broached again if and when he was ready.

As Marc's mother said, 'It is important to be truthful, both to the sick child and to the other children, without having to go into lots of detail.'

Despite being a potentially perplexing age to be, this is not one which troubles greatly about abstract ideas. Not all young children indicate a need to talk about how or when death will come, but by seven years old most of them will know that dead people do not come back. The idea of separation could thus cause most concern.

To die in the heart of the family is to be loved right to the end. To believe that heaven is the home of the Lord Jesus gives the promise of more love and companionship to follow. With such confidence, the lonesomeness of death need hold fewer fears, at any age.

Points to remember for children of about 3–7 years:

*Events are interpreted by what they look like, so illness and some forms of treatment can be seen as punishment.

*New ideas are still matched up with old ones; logical deductions tend to be faulty.

but–

*Experience of a long illness sharpens understanding, so deductions can be more accurate at an earlier age than usual.

*Lack of insight prevents much fearful anticipation, though anxiety may be shown by new physical symptoms as well as in changed behaviour.

*The family is the main source of comfort.

Helpful Bible passages:

Matthew 18:10
Matthew 8:23–27
1 John 4:16–19
Romans 8:35–39

Further reading:

There are many biographies to be found in Christian bookshops, written by parents who have lost a child. Each story is unique, but booksellers would probably advise about books which best suit individual needs.

For parents and professionals:

Lenora Hill (ed.), *Caring for dying children and their families* (London, Chapman and Hall 1994).

For children:

Meryl Doney, *The very worried sparrow* (Oxford, (Lion Publishing plc 1991).

Patricia St John, *Star of light* (London, Scripture Union, seventh reprint 1988).

9

Your death and mine: helping 7–11 year olds

A few days ago I met someone who asked me what I was writing about. When I told him, he said, 'That's interesting. When I was a child, I can clearly remember lying in bed at night, worrying in case I died myself, or what I would do if my parents died.' Although I did not ask him how old he had been then, my guess is that he would have been at the early end of this seven to eleven year old age group.

Starting to make deductions

By now it is well understood, from the television news if not from personal experience, that people die, often in hospital, and that it comes to us all in the end. How to work out the odds as to who, on balance, is likely to go first remains beyond the average capacity of such a young mind.

The youngest children in this group still tend to think in terms of matching things together, so that face-value judgment will also be trailing along. To hear about asthma 'attacks', for example, can conjure up images of guns rather than of illness, though the word may still be used parrot-fashion.

When experience has taught the possibility of some words having two meanings, asking riddles can be great fun, though the inner meanings of parables or proverbs will not usually dawn until the latter end of this age range. Even our Lord's disciples, used to the idea that his stories had double meanings, still had to ask him at times to explain what he meant. In explaining the parable of the sower (Mark 4) the Lord's repeated use of, 'It is like...' is a useful reminder to us that to match up a new idea with one already known is a good basic approach when trying to enlighten anyone.

Arriving at flawed conclusions

The big problem for this age is the tendency to match up two things without considering a vital third element. A seven or eight year old whose brother had died after a long battle with cancer would understandably be very much worried if his father then had to be admitted to hospital. Even though the adults would know that this was for a relatively minor matter, the child would assume the worst unless someone took the trouble to explain.

Personal experience will thus either slant or sharpen understanding. To be told that she has bad blood is likely to convey ideas of naughtiness and blame to a seven year old with leukaemia. It would be better to name her condition outright. Yet an experienced young diabetic often learns quicker than many adults the difference between hypo*glycaemia* (too low a blood sugar) and hyper*glycaemia* (a blood sugar which is too high).

As experience grows, facts can be related in a better sequence, but fantasy is not altogether forgotten. Playground rumour-mongers will embroider a story as it goes round, some no doubt with the help of video nasties. A sick child may hear something new and fearful and, unable to gauge probabilities, could suffer needless apprehension. Many children believe, for instance, that access to the tonsils is gained only by decapitation, so have good reason to dread tonsillectomy. For others to laugh at such misconceptions can make a child feel silly as well as scared, so an adult would do well to sort out these things with a straight face. Fact and fancy may still get confused when a new experience looms, such as a serious illness in the family.

Someone else is dying

When someone is ill or dying, a child under six years old can notice differences in appearance, mood and behaviour, particularly if these are pointed out. Their significance may not be wholly understood until enough time has passed for the child to develop the ability to compare the sick person's past and present abilities. Even then, the child will have only limited awareness of the implications, though there may well be some speculation, particularly as death and dying are so often portrayed by the media. Difficult questions about the expected outcome may arise and can sometimes be on target.

Comparing and contrasting

Recognising fairness and unfairness and feeling sorry for those worse off will now affect a child who is observing someone else's illness. Sympathy can be encouraged if other children in a family see that being ill is not a series of treats. A brother or sister can be tempted to envy the attention given to an ill child until allowed to taste some of the medicine or to watch therapy.

On their good days, the concern of children in an afflicted family is more likely to be expressed in practical and sometimes sacrificial ways. 'I expect he'd like to use my red mug whilst he's ill. He's always said how nice it is.' It may take a child to see most clearly what another child would like. Yet lack of perspective could also mean that such an offer is made to a sick adult as well as to another child.

Forewarning

Because new treatment during a long illness has so far improved things, this pattern will be expected to go on. If this does not happen, children are likely to sense adult anxieties without realising that the changes are now irreversible. Parents or a trusted friend need to be ready to explain what is happening, yet without spelling out the worst too soon. Children, like adults, can face what is actually going on better than they can cope with too vivid an imagination, but explanations need to come step by step.

Long illness, growing minds

When a member of a family is enduring a long illness, perhaps with relapses and then improvements again, each young observer is having time to grow in understanding. A child who was living one day at a time at four years old will eventually start to notice what is going on and begin to ask questions. Past explanations may no longer satisfy but, before updating them, the child's present level of understanding needs to be sensitively explored.

A conversation to clear the air sometimes arises naturally, or could be introduced with, 'Have you noticed anything different about Daddy recently?' An appropriate response could be followed by, 'Why do you think that is?' The answer, 'Perhaps it's because . . .' may indicate the child's grasp of what is happening. Alternatively, the reply, 'Don't know,' could lead on to a simple statement, for example that Daddy's failure to mow the lawn, or even to push out the wheely bin now, is because he is no longer as strong as he was. It is probably best to leave talk about death until either the child asks directly or there is more to be seen to warn of its approach. Once again, for the adult to say, 'I wonder what made you ask me that?' clarifies the question really being asked.

With their varying ages, different children in a family may need a rather different approach. Joanne, aged nine, noticed for herself how Marc, after four years of being ill, was now unable to walk or to see properly and was always tired. Her parents decided to tell her that he would not get better and a little later that he was going to die, 'in case she had little things that she wanted to put right with him.' For this reason, the older child was told earlier than Emma, her four year old sister.

Joanne's family had often moved house, so as well as comparing it to an empty shell (see pages 80, 108), she could think of Marc's body as being like a house. His paralysed legs meant that the house was already falling down and it would not be long before he had to move out. She was not yet experienced enough to be able to imagine what it would be like without him. This limitation spares many children in this age group from the pain which older minds must face.

Choosing to be involved to the end

A year after Marc's funeral, Joanne recalled, 'The thing that made me cry was when the coffin went down. We knew that it was just his body, like his empty house or his empty shell, but it was still sad.' Despite these tears, when asked how she had felt about sharing in this farewell to Marc, she answered simply, 'Very happy.' In more abstract terms than Emma used about heaven, she now visualised him as 'well again, but somewhere else'.

Children are by now well able to see alternatives and express preferences about being part of the family's farewell to someone they have dearly loved. It may be hard for adults to bear to see them there, but that is a different matter.

Is it upsetting to see injuries?

A boy of seven wanted to see his mother, badly injured in a road accident and on a life-support machine. He had been prepared by a pencil and paper sketch for what he would see, but stood very still at the foot of her bed, one tear slowly trickling down his cheek. Later, he asked his father whether his mother was about to 'go up in a box to heaven' and did not want to visit her again. His response did not mean that he should not have seen her, but was a natural reaction to the reality which he had not grasped before. His father reported that the boy slept better after this encounter, with his questions answered, than he had done before it. The mother survived, but if she had died the child would have been prepared.

Involvement denied or enforced

If someone dies suddenly and the body is not seen, a child can think that reports of the death are untrue and that one day the loved one will reappear. A ten year old, experiencing the sudden death of her father in this way, could not for the next four years bring herself to believe that he was really dead. Emotion can overwhelm reason. To deny anyone an encounter with reality can hinder the process of grieving.

'When people come to see the body, you can see the relief on their faces afterwards, even when they'd had to force themselves to go in.' So said our local hospital mortuary attendant, adding, 'I've never known any trouble with children. They seem to accept it better than anyone else.' He added that sometimes he felt that parents were forcing older children to view a body when they would have preferred to wait outside. However, when properly prepared, he had no doubt that it was better for everyone to face the reality than to imagine something far worse. (See also page 103.)

Me, too?

A death in the family can provoke fears in some children that this could be catching, with consequent worry about themselves and others. If an older child in the family has died it is not uncommon for brothers and sisters to expect to die at that same age.

A bright little boy, whose seven year old brother had died when he himself was not yet three, later looked forward with apprehension to being seven. He was very quick to pick up inferences, so when his parents spoke of how one day he, too, would be a Daddy, he at once asked, 'Did you tell Simon about when he'd be a Daddy?' and was clearly relieved when they said, 'No.' The expression of such to and fro ideas may be out of the average for such a young age, but experience as well as intelligence sharpen understanding.

Elizabeth, knowing that she suffered from her sister's fatal disease, remarked on her eighth birthday, 'Am I going to die now, Mummy? I'm eight today and Rachel died when she was eight.' She matched the two facts of diagnosis and age together, but could not possibly gauge the great differences there were in their states of health. Fortunately, she asked and could at that time be reassured. Not all little worriers ask.

Recognising and helping grief

Parents can be very harrassed and preoccupied by the illness of anyone in the family and the upset to normal life which this brings, as well as feeling numb after a death. Events in the lives of their healthy school children, which would normally have aroused interest or praise, may now scarcely get a mention. A child can find it very dull, too, if an old playmate is no longer there and no-one else seems to be free or jolly any more.

The child's feelings can then become a mix of sadness, envy, resentment or plain loneliness and there may be no safe outlet to express them. An understanding family friend, quietly offering a listening ear for the well children as much as for the sick one, could be a great help in relieving tension and restoring focus.

School teachers should be kept in the know about what is happening at home and keep a wary eye open, reporting back any significant observations. Sometimes, children can be made more worried by unexplained tension within the family than about the person who is dying, particularly if this is not someone to whom they feel very close. In their turn, they often grieve over ill, dying or dead school friends more than others in the family may realise.

Significant drawing or writing

A child's doodling or attempts at poetry or prose can often give surprisingly clear clues about what is weighing on the mind. If someone takes the trouble to look, this could start up a helpful conversation. A more direct approach would be to ask openly for such contributions.

After a road accident in which four children were instantly killed, teachers at the local primary school realised that school friends needed to express their grief. After a day or two of shared sorrow, openly expressed by staff and scholars alike, an art class was arranged for the children. It was explained to them that, as it can sometimes be hard to put feelings into words, they were being invited to draw pictures about how they had felt when they heard the sad news.

The idea was taken up willingly and well, some of the young artists weeping a little as they worked, yet without marked distress. Afterwards they freely discussed with their sensitive class teacher what was represented in the drawings. One child had drawn a heart, split in two and dripping tears. Another explained that the boat he had drawn was taking the dead children to heaven. In a radio interview, this teacher and her headmistress said how the classroom experience had not only helped the children. It had also helped each of them to express both personal grief and Christian hope.

Changes in behaviour

As in younger children, behaviour may change and can be helped in the same ways. (See pages 86–92.) Clinginess is especially likely after the death of a parent. The development of dark rings under the eyes, a relapse into a younger level of behaviour, or daydreaming with a fall off in school performance, may all be very natural reactions to sadness.

A child now able to make deductions may have less belief in magic than perhaps she did at three years old, but may still bargain with herself that if she is extra specially good the loved one will get better, or even come back from the dead. Another may continue to act out his confusion and sometimes guilt by being very disruptive. Both these children need a chance to talk over what is happening.

Older children may come across as rigidly controlled, wanting to seem brave and trying not to cause any more trouble. There can also be a fear that other classmates would be embarrassed if they knew how they felt and keep their distance. At the same time, the strain of trying to act normally can bring on troubles which cannot be hidden.

Mind affects body

When inner questions or distress gnaw away unexpressed, physical symptoms can arise even in previously healthy children. Nausea, sickness, poor appetite, tummyache or headache and sometimes bowel or bladder problems can all be indicators of inner tension, as can sleep disturbance and bad dreams. Not uncommonly, some of the symptoms shown by the dying person can affect young children, both before and after the death.

The influence of mind over body is not always realised, particularly in childhood, so parents may understandably fear that the worst is about to happen again. This extra anxiety, picked up by the child, can then make things even worse.

How to help (see also page 89)

The best helper could be a parent, teacher or family friend who is able to offer time and space for some attentive listening. This could happen more naturally by drawing pictures, playing or play-acting together, in play or drama, or by going for a walk or a drive, than by trying to force a face-to-face encounter. Feelings can by now be more easily put into words, or indicated by the various expressions drawn on to the prepared outline of a face. The child will need to be given an opening to unburden without pressure.

There may not yet be sufficient insight for a child to realise just how terrible is the experience being endured or how sympathetic somebody else would be. The misery is made worse by not realising that it is totally understandable.

The body language of affection is unfortunately being inhibited in some schools today, but in a safe atmosphere a caring hug or cuddle from someone who is clearly ready to listen with love can help bottled up feelings to surface and so bring some relief. It can be a great comfort to find that a grown-up shares the sadness and even the tears.

Seeking advice

Advice should be sought early for any child who was present at the time of someone's sudden or violent death. Where there are no distressing visual memories to be played over in the mind, or there has been some preparation, there is less hurry. If symptoms are so severe as to exclude any normal life, or go on without any improvement for more than a week or two, it would be wise to seek advice from the local doctor, nurse or counselling service. It should, of course, be mentioned that there has been a death in the family.

Reassurance that there is no physical illness can itself reduce the symptoms. Putting feelings into pictures, words or prayers will also help.

Even so, it is likely to take anything up to a year or so for a child of this age to put the loss of a close relationship consistently to the back of the mind. Times of brooding can fluctuate with times of normality. If a dead child is later idealised, this adds to the strain for any left behind whose behaviour may, for a time, become either unbelievably good or far from ideal.

The child who is dying

When the child is the one whose death is on its way, adult minds shrink from giving information which, they feel, is going to inflict the pain which they themselves are feeling. The first thing to grasp is that this will not be so. Children at this level of understanding do not have full adult insight. Even though well aware of the fact of death, it is unusual for them to realise its full implications for themselves. Even so, particularly after years of illness during which the mind has had time to change viewpoint, worrying fantasies can arise. This is especially so under the age of eight, before a child has grasped the idea that a dead body no longer feels. We saw in chapter 3 how eight year old Christopher was worrying about his own death for this reason and how anxiety made his wheezing worse until he was helped to unburden.

A child who knows the Lord Jesus as a real friend can inspire others by being so obviously eager to meet him in person. Eight year old Rachel, older sister to Elizabeth, had advanced cystic fibrosis. Two days before her death, she said to her father, 'I love Jesus so much I could put my arms right round him and hug him. I would like to take a present to him when I die.'

Death comes suddenly or slowly

The age span which we are considering in this chapter has the lowest incidence of death in childhood. There is less risk now of the overwhelming infections of infancy. Life-threatening congenital disorders have either taken their toll or are still being treated. The carnage of teenage road accidents still lies ahead. Even so, there is still a mixture of all these causes of death, accompanied by a growing number of childhood malignancies. Serious chest disease from cystic fibrosis is usually, though not always, held at bay for some years yet by new advances in treatment.

Sudden death

This is often precipitated by an accident or follows overwhelming infection. The principles of care remain the same as those discussed earlier (page 114), with known voices and familiar touch being ways of conveying comfort to the end.

Death after a long illness

When a condition has been long-standing, it can come as a surprise to a family when the sufferer suddenly starts to protest at therapy or disability which has previously been accepted without comment. This is simply a sign of the growth of the mind. Comparing and contrasting have taken over from contented 'me-centredness'.

This does not bring the same poignant awareness of being different which can so overwhelm a disabled teenager. It is simply that it has just registered that other people are not putting up with all this, 'so why should I?' This is not always said in so many words, but can instead be acted out in deeds. A sudden refusal to cooperate over hitherto well-tolerated treatment, or a new reluctance to attend hospital, can both indicate this change in outlook.

Helping rebellion

At this point, fresh explanations need to be given to the child as to the nature of the illness and the reason for the treatment. (See also page 122.) Most forms of therapy can be explained in simple terms, given a little medical input, but as the mind can now go to and fro, it may be possible not only to tell but to show a rebel that when treatment is missed symptoms get worse. To be helped to understand is often to become immediately more cooperative.

A boy of seven with cystic fibrosis had to take enzyme tablets to school to help him digest his lunch. As no-one else had to do this, he decided instead to throw them into the litter bin. He then lost weight, so was found out. A fuller explanation than he had grasped before led to better cooperation and the lost weight was regained.

Deterioration

A child who has seen the benefits of treatment will also be able to see when it is no longer working. Feeling steadily less well, or knowing that certain test results are getting worse, both begin to tell a clear story. This does not yet bring the same fear to the hearts of children as it can do for older people. If encouraged, they may well talk openly about death rather than asking indirect questions about it. When queries do arise, they can as readily be posed to someone outside the family as to a close relative.

Transplants

Several advanced diseases of childhood can be helped by organ or bone marrow transplantation. This should be discussed with the child, who is by now able to compare two options and share decisions. At a specialist transplant centre, children will also have had a chance to compare notes and to realise that this is usually a matter of life and death.

Rachel was seven years old when she developed leukaemia. Two years later she underwent a bone marrow transplant in a hospital 200 miles from her home. Her admission there lasted for three months, much of the time in an isolation tent. It was also during this period that her mother had another baby, so her father's allegiance was divided between the two units.

Rachel had undergone gruelling preparation for a bone marrow transplant earlier that year, but the disease had relapsed before it was done. She hesitated about a second attempt and for a time refused to agree to it. There was no doubt that she knew that without it she would die and could do so soon anyway. It was probably for her parents' sake that she finally gave her consent. Within two weeks of getting home after it had been done, the disease was rampant again and three weeks later Rachel died, a few weeks before her tenth birthday.

I only met this lovely child for half an hour a few weeks before her death. She was wrapping up Christmas parcels and was delighted to tell me how, as soon as she woke up on Christmas morning, she always wished the Lord Jesus a happy birthday. She was full of his praises for helping her with the ordeal of the transplant saying, 'I just couldn't have got through it all without the Lord.'

A child's legacy

In the isolation tent, Rachel had kept two little notebooks, which she gave me to read. In one she had recorded her bad thoughts and in the other her good ones. The second little book contained poems and prayers which revealed quite clearly the importance to her of relationships, both human and heavenly, and her concern for all those who did not know her Lord.

One prayer was entitled, 'Without you', and it read, 'Without Mum and Dad I don't know what I would do, I mean I wouldn't have anyone to love or care for. Without you, Lord my Saviour, I wouldn't have been able to go through with all my treatment. So please Saviour, my Saviour, please help me and all the other people, so please, please help us, our Saviour. Amen.'

Rachel's care for others, despite her own need, was remarkable. Her father later said what a lot he had learned from her. 'When I was at school they taught us religion like any other subject. Rachel showed me that it is really about a relationship.'

Another Rachel, as she died of cystic fibrosis, was also able to comfort her parents. In her last hours, she smiled many delighted smiles and then asked them, 'Why couldn't you see them singing?' When her father asked what she could see she answered, 'Jesus'. She then somehow found the strength to get off her bed and hug each parent in turn before letting go of life in her father's arms.

Later he, too, had a comment to make: 'The last hour of Rachel's life on earth was undoubtedly the happiest hour of her life. God graciously allowed us to see the miracle for which we had prayed (though not in the way we had expected). Her smiles of delight and, we believe, recognition, should give us all assurance of our hope. This was not passing from life into death, but from death into life.'

It is not given to all children to have such a joyful departure. Shortly before losing consciousness, the Rachel dying of leukaemia asked why God was allowing her to suffer so much. Yet one of her poems tells how she had dreamed of the angels taking her up to heaven to see God. 'We spoke. He told me that he wanted to make the world a better place.' She then woke up, her poem says, with an 'unexsblainable' feeling.

The legacy of her writing blesses us, too. Even through her suffering the world can hear of the love of God and, if responsive to him, become the better place she dreamed about.

Points to remember for children of about 7–11 years old:
*Judging by appearances lingers on.
*Although learning to put two and two together, wrong conclusions are likely.
*If an illness spans these years and cooperation falters, the child's changed outlook may be the cause.
*Anxiety and grief can cause physical symptoms and behavioural change.
*Faith can be real and expressed.

Helpful Bible passages:
2 Corinthians 12:7–10
Hebrews 12:1–3

Further reading and viewing.
For parents and professionals:
Christine Eiser, *Growing up with a chronic disease* (London, Jessica Kingsley Publishers 1993).
Janet Goodall, *Facing chronic illness and death when the patient is a child.*
Video available from Graves Medical AV Library, Concord Video and Film Council, 201, Felixstowe Road, Ipswich IP3 9BJ

For children:
Patricia St John, *The Tanglewoods' Secret* (London, Scripture Union, eighth reprint

1992). Video version: International Films (Amersham, Scripture Press).

10

Your death and mine: helping adolescents

'Being thirteen is a joy beyond all bounds . . . being a teenager at last! Everyone seems to think that once you are a teenager you are grown up and should be treated like an adult. This is not true, of course, but it's nice to have people say adult things instead of taking you by the hand. When you say you're a teenager to other teenagers older than you, they seem to stop the teasing and the jeering and want to be friends.'

So wrote Andrew in a school examination paper. He touches on several things held dear to the whole of this group, of which freedom from oppressive adult control and the good opinion of friends rank high. Although the emphasis in this chapter is on teenagers, much of it will also apply to many twelve year olds.

Normally, young people are now beginning to think in the same three dimensional way as adults do. They are able to look back and make more appropriate deductions, to look ahead with more accurate expectation and also have greater self-awareness and insight. As Andrew said himself, this does not imply that teenagers themselves are now mature, but their method of thinking has matured.

Despite all this, the physical and emotional growth spurt going on at the same time often upsets orderly thought. The adolescent bid for independence can produce conflict with others which sometimes is as difficult to live with as toddler negativism. Negotiations can replace cooperation and home can become a kind of garage, used chiefly as a source of fuel, valet service and shelter.

Yet underneath all this lies the desire which has been there from birth, which is to be committed to mutually loving and lasting relationships. As the circle of friendship grows, the influence of friends grows, too. Deep down, though, family ties may be stronger than they can sometimes seem.

Growing up into grief

Grief may add pain to pain for this age group, or bring sudden clouds to clear skies. No longer wanting to be 'taken by the hand', freedom of choice is important to adolescents. This needs to be applied when deciding how much to be involved when someone else is dying or has died. Grief tends to follow adult lines (described in chapter 1), though sometimes with fewer inhibitions.

Sudden death

The sudden loss of anyone in the family, perhaps particularly a much loved parent, can bring an overwhelming sense of disbelief. This will be mixed with guilt if rebellious things have been said or done. There is a sense of losing control again when freedom from family restraints was only just beginning. This can be acted out in unusual behaviour.

A teenager whose sister dropped dead in the street from a brain haemorrhage took to staying out late and being rude and nasty when he came in. His parents' first reaction was to ask each other, 'How can he behave like this, worrying us silly when we are so upset already?' In fact, he was showing the alienation and anger of his own grief.

In another school essay, Sarah, aged fifteen, wrote, 'Benjy and I always had a special bond. The day of the accident he met me at the gate with loves and kisses when I came home from school. Then we set out to deliver some papers. Suddenly there was a bang and my little Ben was flying down the road. At that moment, I remembered his words of the day before, asking if we'd promise to let him stay four for ever. Then I was running screaming down the road. Although he was still and pale, he still looked so beautiful. It was then that I knew he would always be four.'

An hour or two later, I met Sarah in the Accident Unit, where efforts to resuscitate Ben were still going on. It was as if a sword had pierced her. She scarcely heard me say that the accident had not been her fault. The force of her guilt and grief were to turn inwards and affect her physical and emotional health for years. During those years, she trained to become a nursery nurse.

Death on an intensive care unit

In her devastated recognition that Ben would die, Sarah found it too hard to stay there as vain attempts were made to bring him back. For others, it can give more time to adjust to the idea of what is happening. Some young people could feel less out of control if told something about the equipment in use and its purpose before moving in any closer. Terrifying technology could otherwise cause panic.

Others would value being invited to comb the hair, wash the face or simply to whisper personal messages to their loved one. Closer contact would gradually make it clearer that death was on its way. Such an involved presence should not be forced, but can be offered in a matter-of-fact way, perhaps more successfully by a nurse of about the same age. I was once discussing with someone how important it is for very little children, who cannot imagine what is happening, to visit close relatives on such units. He looked very dubious and said, 'Well, when I was on the intensive care unit, my son came in to see me, took one look and ran out of the room.' The obvious question was, 'How old was he?' The answer came back, 'Fourteen.' Thanks in part to what he may have gleaned from television, a fourteen year old would be much more aware than a younger child of the serious implications of his father's condition. Toddlers and teenagers are different and their very different needs have to be appreciated before they can be met in appropriately different ways.

Sharing someone's slower death

When there is more warning that someone in the family has a terminal disease, a young person is now going to be quick to notice changes, to pick up innuendos and work out implications. It would therefore be wise to share bad news early, whilst not destroying the hope of some good times still to come. This can bolster confidence and cement relationships.

When a parent or older relative is dying, there may be quiet talks about unfinished tasks which a youngster may like to take up, or a few last wise words about career or other plans. This is all likely to depend on the openness and strength of the earlier relationships. Different personalities may cope, or not cope, in varied ways, but there are those who say that adolescents weather the loss of a loved one better than anyone else.

Being a Christian is no guarantee of a serene death. Sometimes the younger generation can support the faith of their elders when advancing physical weakness threatens to bring depression of mind and spirit. As a young girl, my grandmother lost within days both her parents and a baby brother, from smallpox. As they lay dying, she and her sisters looked up encouraging Bible passages and read them aloud, through the cottage window.

Helpful ways to think about death

Being able now to think in abstract terms opens up more helpful imagery. Death can be compared with birth, or with going to sleep on a journey and waking up somewhere else. The idea of death as sleep is no longer the alarming image it would have been earlier.

These comparisons will be most helpful of all when seen to be an earthly image with a heavenly truth. Just as an unborn but already loved baby has to face a struggle before being able to gaze into the parents' faces, so any who are in a living relationship with God will, on passing through death, enter more fully into what it means to know him as they see him face to face. Promises to do with the ultimate resurrection of the body can now be clearly distinguished from popular ideas about reincarnation.

A young person's sadness over another's death

The emotions of denial and anger or guilt, depression and bargaining often whirl about wildly, just as they can do for adults. Yet, as with younger children, grief has to be recognised before it can be helped.

Denial and anger (See also page 13)

Staying at a distance or showing disturbed behaviour may follow the shock of a sudden death in the immediate circle. Suicidal feelings or even attempts are not unusual, especially if guilt or emptiness predominate.

As Judy Baer illustrates in her book *Tomorrow's promise*, isolation, anger and guilt can all arise when a loved one's personality changes, as with Alzheimer's disease.

A young person may also hold on strongly to inner disbelief in the face of all the evidence when someone is clearly dying. This can be a form of God-given anaesthetic but, like all other anaesthesia, it must come to an end when its work is done.

God will heal her if I pray hard enough

This was my own secret hope during my mother's last illness. During those months, I was preparing for the examinations on which my entrance to medical school would depend. Although she had discussed her approaching death with me, I clung to this mixture of denial and bargaining. No doubt aided by my parents' own prayers, this carried me successfully through the examinations. Ten days after my eighteenth birthday, our doctor enlisted my help with my mother's last injection of morphine. At last, I was able to acknowledge her suffering and say, 'Lord, you can take her if this is your will.' A few hours later, that is just what he did.

Friends may seem to mean more than family

Even in the devastation of losing someone as close as a parent, twin, or close friend there may be some unwillingness to turn for comfort to the family circle, for fear of again being treated like a child. Many find support in a close mate, whilst others turn to nobody at all.

A bereaved family can interpret this as, 'He doesn't seem to care. He just goes out all the time with his friends', or, 'She's always going up to mope in her room'. These are, in fact, both forms of licking the wounds. A wise teacher, older family friend or trusted youth group leader may be able to get alongside more readily than anyone in the family. Someone trying to help a young person to unburden needs to approach this both cautiously and casually. It is worth remembering that teenagers often love a heart to heart chat by telephone, though more so when they already have a good relationship with someone.

If a brother or sister is dying, it is good to keep other friendships alive. They are necessary now as well as being important later. Young people need to feel helpful, but need also to be freed from feeling that their unfailing presence at the bedside is either expected or essential.

Twins

When the dying person is also a twin, there are sure to be complicated emotions for the one who will be left with a new and unique sense of being alone. Whilst leaving such a pair to choose their own degree of involvement with each other there needs, too, to be recognition of the high level of mutual distress. A tactful offer of sensitive and skilled help may or may not be gratefully welcomed.

New responsibilities after a death

Almost immediately after a parent's death, older boys may find themselves pushed into becoming the man of the household, or girls similarly expected to be instant housewives. Alternatively, the family's affairs may be taken in hand by another friend or relative who makes decisions without any consultation. Both these extremes can promote quiet desperation or angry outbursts. It would be very different for a teenager to be enabled to assume a newly-vacated responsibility voluntarily. To have one's opinion sought, for example about hymns for the funeral, is also better than being made to feel once more subservient, or merely swept up in arrangements made by others.

On the other hand, many adolescents instinctively and at once become strongly supportive to a surviving parent or to the remaining members of a bereft family. This is probably the age where reactions are least foreseeable and can also quickly change.

Attending rites of passage

Implications can now be foreseen and there is also better self-awareness. A teenager may therefore fear that too close an involvement could prove too much for the now important but fragile self-control. This can lead to at least an initial decision not to see the body, although with the option of a change of mind later on if reassured by others.

The need to appear adult or supportive, as well as simply to show affection, usually leads to attendance at the funeral. To be there with a trusted friend can bolster confidence, so that an older teenager may even be able take some part in the service, such as reading a lesson.

Public grief

After the death of someone much loved, the period of mourning is likely to go on for many months and is made longer and more complex when it began without warning. To the attuned eye, many of the features of grief are obvious, but cannot be hurried away. Sufferers need patience and understanding, not exhortations to accept God's will or to try and be a bit more cheerful.

Other mourners may show personality changes which could mystify those who know little about grief or its immediate and long-term effects. Shervanthi was an eleven year old Sri Lankan child who was full of mischief and with a reputation for high spirited naughtiness. Early one morning, six weeks after the arrival of a little brother, their mother suddenly died. At once, Shervanthi changed into a serious and self-sacrificing little mother to the baby. She grew up to become a respected surgeon, and still gives herself to the needs of others to the point of exhaustion.

Private grief can last

As Jill Fuller tells us in her book about John, open sympathy from school-mates can now be embarrassing. Whilst attempting an adult public face by day, tears may be saved for the pillow or for the sympathetic friend. They can go on for a year or more and then still cause surprise when something relatively small triggers them off again, even years later. Someone may innocently ask about a dead father's job. Another death, even one out of the family, or of a pet, can rekindle the old sorrow. Weeping with those who weep may always come easily.

In her interviews with such young people, Jill Krementz found that they found comfort in meeting someone else who had been through the same experience. Surviving twins find it particularly helpful to meet other lone twins.

A loss experienced long ago can still raise questions as the maturing mind reflects on the past. Nearly fifteen years after her brother Marc's death, when she was four years old, Emma would now like to know more details about how he died. She remembers seeing his body, but not crying much then. 'Seeing the coffin go down is when I realised that he was never coming back. I do remember crying at this point and still when I picture the moment in my mind, I feel a deep sadness. Looking back I'm so glad I went to the funeral. If I hadn't, I'm sure I wouldn't have accepted his death as well as I did.

'I think that having coped with his death, it made me more able to deal with the grief I felt when my Nana died.'

It may not be long after someone dear to them has died that young people have to move away to a job, or start studies at a university. They will not

always mention the bereavement to new friends, but the Christian network is such that a welcome into an understanding home can be a great solace. I speak from experience!

Adolescents facing their own death

The increased dependency imposed by illness or disability can now be the hardest part to bear, often added to by loss of good looks and self-esteem.

After an accident

By far the majority of teenage deaths are from road accidents or their results. From the pinnacle of independence, life is snuffed out or descends into what to a survivor may seem like endless and humiliating disability. This is grief indeed, well described already by Joni Earickson in books written some years after breaking her neck in a diving accident. Now paralysed and in a wheelchair, she describes not only what it is like at the bottom of the pit of despair but how God gently lifted her up and out of it again.

Changes in appearance

The fact that much life saving therapy is also disfiguring should be spelt out in advance, but it can still come as a blow when it happens. The prolonged use of steroids in high dosage is one example. It helps a young person to be able to look back on a consciously made decision, arrived at by weighing up the pros and cons of blemished survival or inevitable death and choosing the first. Unprepared for what lay ahead, a twelve year old I once knew exercised the fragments of his independence by refusing to go on with therapy which, he felt, was not worth what it was costing him.

A greater sense of being in control can be given by the offer of more choice over the dates of the treatment, the injection sites, or of drugs which seem to help most. A hairpiece may be needed after cytotoxic therapy and the wearer can help to design it. Making more basic choices, such as what to eat, wear or do, also gives back a measure of independence.

Disabled from birth

A problem which has been lived with from birth can now be slowly deteriorating. Boys with some forms of muscular dystrophy are likely to die in their teens as are some young people with other progressive diseases, though new techniques can now prolong life for many with, for example, cystic fibrosis or heart disease.

Young people with disabilities are not as dismayed and upset by their condition as many able-bodied people are on their behalf. I once heard one of them say, 'You may be sorry for me, being in a wheelchair, but to me this chair spells freedom.'

This is not to dismiss the anguish of unrequited love, or the pain of other harsh truths, which some have shared with me. Although many of these difficulties form a part of what it means to be human, there is still a special pain to be borne when an adolescent with a disability first faces its personal implications. If this includes the realisation that life is running out, there is likely to be the same mix of feelings as anyone else would face.

Nowadays, there looms for some the question of organ transplantation, adding uncertainty to uncertainty. This means, too, that ongoing aggressive therapy may go beyond the stage where gentler terminal care would normally have been started. One who has had lifelong therapy aimed at cure will know the difference when the goal and the treatment change. To play a part in deciding about one's own management again gives back a degree of control.

Malignant disease

Much the same pattern, of gradual decline and failing therapy, holds for young people dying of cancer, leukaemia or one of the other malignancies. Honesty, trust and warm support, established from the time of diagnosis onwards, are of enormous value.

When seeking to hold on to some control, even when dying, some young people want to be clearer about what lies ahead and then get ready to face it. I had to tell Anthony, aged twelve, that his cancer treatment was not working. There seemed to be little point in his putting up with its side-effects any more. 'Well, that's it then,' he said, 'My life's in God's hands and it's up to him what happens now.'

Such a serene coming to terms with illness or

death does not always come readily. Barbara was found to have bone cancer when thirteen years old and it was decided to amputate her leg. With hindsight it seems that she had not clearly understood why this had been done.

Previously she had been a very sporty girl, but now felt deserted by her old friends. She had problems in adjusting to the artificial leg, with all that it now denied her. Then someone bluntly asked her, 'What is it like to have cancer, Barbara?' Suddenly grasping the diagnosis and all its possible implications, she took an overdose and was admitted to the ward where I worked so we all got to know her.

Like many other teenagers, she found it hard to communicate closely with her mother, a lone parent who needed to work. During the next eighteen months Barbara was in hospital for weeks at a time. She had anti-cancer therapy and more surgery. She and her mother received counselling. She was banned from school for repeated solvent sniffing, which continued secretly in hospital. Very fashion conscious, she wore long skirts to hide her amputation and for a time favoured the punk style. If life was to be short it was certainly colourful.

Yet Barbara sometimes said how sad she was to have no close friends and how she did not feel free to talk about her illness to her mother lest she upset her. In turn, her mother, who was a very private person, was scared to talk about the illness lest Barbara took another overdose. Each was locked into her own emotional prison and as the disease spread, it seemed that it was a race against time to bring them into any greater freedom.

Three months before she died, Barbara said quite openly, 'I'm not afraid of death, or what will happen afterwards and I'm not afraid of pain, but just of being out of control.' She also said how much she still longed to be open with her mother and when the vicar called asked him to pray for them.

Barbara slowly grew weaker. Less than a month before her death, her mother let it be known in an unusually heated exchange that she thought Barbara's reserve was based on 'hating me that much'. In pained surprise, her daughter replied, 'But I don't hate you.' Although each later had misgivings about this episode, it had at last opened up honest communication between them.

On the very last day of her life, scarcely able to speak, Barbara asked to go home. Once there, in privacy and for the first time, she lovingly put her arms round her mother, who later said that she had never seen her look so happy.

The vicar came to pray with them before mother and daughter spent that last night together, 'and it was the best night of our lives.' Their relationship had been restored, only just in time.

Such a story tells something of the possible turmoil of grief, going on within and around a dying adolescent. Not all find the road so hard, but neither do all reach what they long for before their journey ends.

Windows into the mind

Skilled counselling was needed to help Barbara and her mother. Others can more easily say, write or show through artwork or drama how they feel, sometimes as members of a group. Dreams can be revealing. Young (and older) Christians may need opportunity to discuss the problem of pain. Many prefer to be private.

Clare, dying of cystic fibrosis, spoke quietly to her mother about heaven. She also painted a delicate, solitary flower on a long, slim stem, reaching up towards the blue sky. Its petals, we noted later, were heart-shaped.

Physical death, spiritual life

I have not yet looked after a dying teenager who was not searching for spiritual life when facing physical death, though this may not at first have been clear. Those who do not easily express this should not be forced into conversation. Others may give clear clues that their trouble is not entirely physical or emotional, but spiritual as well.

Behavioural change

Nigel was a boy I looked after years ago. He developed lung cancer when only fourteen years old, which ended his cherished hopes of service in the Navy. Normally a peaceable lad, in his anguish he chased his mother round the kitchen with a carving knife. She was a Christian woman and must have prayed hard! Her prayers were answered, as Nigel finally gave his allegiance to the Lord, talked to his sisters about his coming death and led his father to faith before dying in peace, at home.

Obvious anxiety

Jill, a seventeen year old with advanced cystic fibrosis, came into hospital very breathless and sleeping badly after hearing of the death of her friend, Clare, from the same disease. Despite new and stronger therapy and support from her very caring family, including visits from her much loved sheepdog, she remained breathless and anxious.

Her doctor realised that Jill's physical deterioration and emotional state went together, but also that her own fear of death was contributing to both, so he asked her an unusually direct question. Although not an avowed believer himself, he had the sensitivity to say, 'Do you believe in God, Jill?' to which she answered, 'Yes.' 'Well,' said this perceptive man, 'I don't know much about him myself, but I'll find someone for you who does.' As he said later, those without religious beliefs themselves need to recognise how important faith must be to those who hold it dear.

Accordingly, the hospital chaplain and I in turn listened to Jill's questions. She wanted to know how Clare had died, and was assured that she had been made comfortable and had not been alone. The presence of the sheepdog led on to speak naturally of the Good Shepherd and his promise to be with us at all times, even in dark valleys.

Gradually, over the next few days, Jill became calmer until, like her friend Clare before her, she died peacefully one morning with her loved ones around her. Whilst still holding her dead daughter in her arms, her mother looked up and said, 'Is it really true? Has the Shepherd got her safe?' The answer, 'Yes', was given in faith; for faith is being sure of what we hope for and certain of what we do not see (Hebrews 11:1).

Looking beyond and thinking of others

Anthony, now dying of cancer, would sometimes lie quietly meditating. He once opened his eyes and said to his mother, 'If I die, I don't want you worrying yourself and losing weight. I'll be all right with Jesus in heaven. It's you lot down here I'll be sorry for.' His serene trust drew both his parents to faith at the time of his death.

Some young people during their last illness like to make out a will. Elizabeth, dying of cystic fibrosis at thirteen years old, also helped to prepare her own funeral service. Amongst other verses, she chose one which was first said by the Lord Jesus. It still speaks to any with minds able now to range ahead, to wonder, and to seek and find his reassurance:

'I will be with you always, to the very end of the age.' (Matthew 28:20)

Points to remember about adolescence:

*Adolescents prize independence.

*Whatever their behaviour, they long for committed, loving relationships.
*Their way of thinking may be adult, but emotion often overrides reason.
*Grief follows the adult pattern.
*A dying teenager may well want to know what kind of death to expect and also to seek spiritual assurance of life to come.

Helpful Bible passages:
John 11:23–27
Revelation 7:13–17

Further reading for young (or order) people:

Joni Eareckson with Steve Estes, *A step further* (London, Pickering and Inglis 1979).

Jill Fuller, *John's book* (Cambridge, The Lutterworth Press 1993).

C. S. Lewis, *The last battle* (London, Lions, HarperCollins 1956).

Further reading for parents and professionals:

Beverley Raphael, 'The adolescent's grief and mourning', chapter 4 in *The anatomy of bereavement* (London, Century Hutchinson Ltd 1984).

11

Roses have thorns but thorns have roses

Perhaps, like me, you have heard people complain about our Lord, 'First he says "Suffer the little children to come to me" and then he makes them suffer. What kind of a God is that?'

Where is God when it hurts?

In this final chapter I want to face this question with you. I am a children's doctor, not a theologian, so I shall first look for my answer to the loving Lord who called the children to his arms when he was here. Then I shall look to some of the children I have known whom he has called to go to him since.

First, though, we must correct the notion so broadly hinted at in the question, that true love would not allow suffering. I have often had to hurt my little patients, not because I did not care about them, but because caring meant action and sometimes, when doctors act, it can hurt. It also hurts to cause pain. Consenting parents, too, suffer as they watch what is going on, unable to stop it or even to kiss it better. Love and suffering can be very much intertwined.

God with us

In Alister McGrath's little book, *Suffering*, he comments, 'One of the chief glories of the Christian faith is the way in which it links love and suffering. How is the love of God shown? Supremely through the suffering and death of Jesus Christ.'

The most loving act that God ever did was a most painful one, disruptive for the whole Godhead, and it was done voluntarily, out of love for us. When we feel torn apart he knows what it is like, for he has been there, too.

Made in his image

To think of the interrelationships within the Godhead gives us an inkling of what can be implied when the Bible talks of our being made in God's image. I have often thought of this when seeing new babies and their parents getting together. Their immediate mutual attraction and growing love for each other is a little picture of how God has designed us to relate not only to each other, but also to him. Just as a restless baby who has learned to love will give an ecstatic welcome back to someone who has been away, so our hearts will be restless until they find their rest in him.

The opposite of this delight is the sad emptiness which follows when relationships are damaged or broken. We saw earlier how this was reflected in the faces of desolate little Ugandans and other infants in Eastern Europe as they lost appetite and wasted away when cut off from love. To be out of relationship with God has the same effect on the soul. When this happens, it is not he who has abandoned us but we who have departed from him.

As my own heart sank to see those bereft children, so his love and pity are stirred to see the state of those who do not know him. His power could force them to come back to him. Instead his love brought him into the world to join them, hoping to inspire a welcoming response. For humanity to join up with him again would be to restore once more his lost image in each of us but, even when he was here, only a few chose this way. Others conspired to reject and to kill him.

This is part of the message of the cross of Christ: the upright signals his huge descent and the cross-bar his arms outstretched in a self-giving act of yearning love. In his love and pity he came to redeem us. This was the price he was prepared to pay to draw us back into the shelter of his love and so to save our shrivelling souls. We can respond with delight, turning to him in responsive love and being revitalised, or we can turn away to pursue our own ends and so meet our own end. He gives us freedom to choose.

Even a very little child can learn that 'Jesus loves

me'. This was my own experience at five years old when, like a lost lamb, I heard the call of the Good Shepherd and responded to his love. Yet just as children have to grow up in their thinking, so do Christians.

Guarantee, not insurance

It may be hard to hear this when already crying out in pain, but the Christian life is not a bed of roses and following our Lord is no insurance policy against suffering. Both the story of Job and the apostle Paul's thorn in the flesh (mentioned in 2 Corinthians 12:7) remind us that for as long as we live in this world, Christians will not be excused some of its unpleasant experiences. This can include a share of personal grief and suffering. 'Why us?' can be changed to, 'Why not us?'

God is with us in the pain

Just as most parents stand by their suffering children, so our heavenly Father is alongside to help. Sometimes he brings about physical healing. Often, though, it seems that his transforming grace and strength are quietly at work, even when outward suffering and inner isolation continue.

To turn away from him now is to find desolation made more desolate. There comes a time, even with all our doubts and questions, when there is nowhere else to turn for any hope and comfort, but to him. One day we shall know as we are known. Meantime, knowledge grows largely through trust.

Growing pains

Let me digress for a moment to take you into my garden. I am no gardener, so at first I was rather alarmed when my friend and neighbour started to do what seemed to me terrible things to my rose bushes, leaving me with thorns but no roses. Yet when summer came I could see what had been in his mind. The same thoughts may have inspired Faber, whose words give this chapter its title.

Long months after the pruning, new buds burst into abundant and beautiful life. The lacerated branches were transformed and the thorns had roses again. With them, I was given a lesson in trust. My friend had known what he was doing as he picked up his secateurs.

The Lord Jesus, as recorded in John 15, compared his Father to an even more skilful gardener, whose intention is for us not only to love, trust and know him better, but for our lives to produce an abundance of fruit. We would be happy enough simply to let this be the love, joy and peace produced by his presence in our lives, but he wants to see patience, longsuffering, gentleness and self-control growing in us as well.

God may not approve that which he allows

I am not intending to suggest that, for creative purposes of his own, God therefore deliberately wills the Chernobyl cancers, the Bosnian bullets or the horrors of civil war in Rwanda. There is a distinction to be drawn between God's perfect will and his permissive will. He allows inhuman wickedness only because he allows human freedom, but he must feel intensely pained by what that freedom brings. We must not equate the outrages committed by man on man with a father's training of his beloved children. Discipline comes through firm affection, not from fearful abuse.

Although, in my limited understanding of his ways, I cannot think that he designs all that he allows, I believe that it is part of the meaning of the cross that he takes hold of human griefs and sorrows to redeem them. He can use all the circumstances of our lives as instruments for good. The gardener and the surgeon do not manufacture all their instruments but they know how to use them. So does he.

The only possible security when some of the world's grief comes home is to offer relief where we can, but trust the outcome to him. This can be so even when life seems to hold no meaning and when the worst part of it is that the pain is hitting hardest those we love the most.

Follow me

The Lord Jesus himself warned us that to follow him would be costly. Whatever is involved in this for individuals, be it persecution, unfulfilled ambition or personal anguish of some other kind, it can be a way to identify with his suffering and to find his strength. After the pattern of the cross, this will often mean being willing, in total humility, to make an offering of the crushing trouble to him, wanting above all else to bring honour to his name as we do so.

As the gloom of the first Easter Saturday gave way to the joy of Easter Sunday, so this can become our own hope as we trudge through the darkest valleys in the footsteps of our risen Lord. We may look forward with longing to the promised resurrection of our bodies in the future, but dare also hope for some reshaping of our brokenness whilst still in this present life.

In following the Lord Jesus, not only are we to learn from him and to lean on him; his intention is for us to become like him and we are offered the power of his resurrection to transform us. His Holy Spirit longs to change us into a replica of his likeness. What could be better than that?

Making or breaking?

Yet sometimes it seems that times of trial can break us apart rather than being used to make us more beautifully Christlike. Some blame an experience of suffering for their loss of faith and the total void that this then brings. Depression can breed isolation. It is hard to look outwards or upwards when the eyes are filled with tears.

Perhaps some who feel such disillusion have been reading this book, looking for help with your own grief and that of your grieving children whilst feeling like hurt children yourselves. You long for the comfort of a loving heavenly Father's arms but instead feel severed from him by deep and dreadful cuts which he has allowed and which, you may feel, have set you apart from each other, perhaps for ever. For a time this may be all you can do, to feel like a child crying in the dark and longing for the familiar presence to come back. He has not ceased to exist because he is allowing you to suffer, neither has he ceased to care. In truth, he is not far from any one of us and if we feel after him, the intention is that we shall find him (Acts 17:27).

Can there be any meaning in it all?

There is no easy answer to the problem of pain and suffering, made all the more poignant when the one at the heart of it is so young. The goad of such human tragedy has forced many parents to search for some kind of meaning as they have struggled in their own families to support a dying or disabled child. Most would say that they will never be the same again. A few are sure that the gaping scar will never close. Many also confess with wonder that they feel strangely enriched, even after sustaining such terrible loss.

Margaret Spufford in *Celebration*, Mary Craig in *Blessings* and Frances Young in *Face to faith* all speak about insights learned through their own special trials. As each book's title suggests, despite the individual stories being so overwhelmingly painful, the experience for each of these mothers has also been transforming.

A celebration of holy communion

Margaret Spufford suffered with her 'humanely treated, routinely tormented' daughter through years of painful investigation and treatment at a leading children's hospital. She writes: 'On those terrible children's wards I could neither have worshipped nor respected any God who had not himself cried, "My God, my God, why hast Thou forsaken Me?" Only because it was so, only because the Creator loved His creation enough to become helpless with it and suffer in it, totally overwhelmed by the pain of it, I found there was still hope.' She goes on to quote Hebrews 2:18, a reminder that because our Lord himself suffered, he is able to help those who suffer now; 'but not, in my experience by removing the suffering. The beauty of the twisted tree is still brought out *through* its contortion.' Our part is to offer him the contortions of our lives as a living sacrifice and later to be amazed at what he has been able to do in accepting these costly offerings. This is what deepens communion and deserves celebration.

Kept by the power of God

The fellowship of suffering with Christ should be linked strongly (as in Philippians 3:10) with the power of his resurrection. Many personal stories bear testimony to the reality of this power, even in such simple terms as, 'I just don't know how we got through it.' Others say that the reality which stopped them from going under was supportive love, often channelled through other people, who perhaps without knowing it conveyed the personal care and power of God. We remain precious to him and he is still with us, in the midst of the fieriest of trials.

Comfort overflows

To speak of fellowship in suffering also reminds us of those who know what it means to have been badly hurt themselves, yet later reach out to help others who still feel helpless and hurt. As was the pattern of the cross, it is in costly commitment to the good of others, wanting in spite of everything to help someone else, that all our relationships can eventually become creative. Each can help to raise the other, not in our own strength, but by the dynamic inner power of his Holy Spirit.

But what about the children themselves?

I, too, often agonise over this question and what I have to say next is said hesitantly, lest it sound forced. Yet the children have something to say which it would be quite wrong to stifle.

Even in the blackness of Bosnia, our television screens have shown us at least one child who mutely gritted her teeth as her wounds were dressed so that her little brother would not be frightened. In the terrible Rwandan refugee camps, we have watched older orphans reach out a hand to the younger ones. Love is not easily quenched. Small candles shine more brightly in the dark.

Later on, the cared for can become carers. We traced this earlier in the book, when we sometimes saw how those who had been hurt as children grew up to take care of others. The textbooks call this 'compulsive caring' as though it were something unnatural, and it is true that some can stretch themselves too far. Yet perhaps such care can also be supernatural. Our gracious God is able to heal the wounded in spirit and leave them sensitised to the needs of others.

We saw, too, how other children, even when dying, showed a thoughtfulness for other people which was beyond their years. Rachel, suffering from leukaemia in an isolation tent, prayed for 'all the other people' as well as asking for the Saviour's help for herself.

Anthony, being carried out for the last time from his home, was badly jarred as someone stumbled. He yelped in pain, making his father turn on the ambulance men in anger. A quiet voice came from the stretcher, 'Don't be cross with them Dad; they didn't mean it.' I am reminded of one who also said, 'Forgive them, Father.'

At times, the secret strength of some children was made all the more telling when they spoke openly and confidently of the love between them and their Lord. We heard another Rachel say how she wanted to give Jesus a hug when she met him, and that was to be soon. Whatever it may look like, the love of the Lord Jesus and the reality of his presence can be a child's experience, right to the end.

Sometimes this love has drawn others, as we saw when some of the parents decided to follow their children as they had followed Christ. Even young people who made no such open profession could show in their dying how their priorities were not with things, but with people.

Yes, suffering children can sometimes show us how we ought to be. God can use for good even that which seems so bad. We may cry out in protest, sometimes in anger and often in bewilderment, but perhaps part of the answer is being spelled out before us, even as we do so. There may not yet be enough light to read by, but in waiting on him the long darkness can slowly be turned to a clearer dawning.

God is not in a hurry

Earlier, in chapter 5, I spoke of a baby, David, whose parents took him home with inoperable spina bifida. He died in their loving care after only a few weeks. Some years later, I saw them again with another child and it became clear then that they were Christians. 'We weren't Christians, though, when we had David,' they told me, 'although we thought we were. It was because we'd had him that people in our church started to pray for us and that's how it all happened.' I had learned a lot from them as well as from the first Christian couple whose example they had followed. These two families had turned around a hospital's previous policy and helped many parents afterwards to take their dying babies home. Quite unconsciously they had thus helped others, so it was heartwarming to hear in turn how God had blessed them, even through their pain.

In the year that David died, five year old Marc died, too. We have all shared something of the lessons learned by accompanying him, his parents and his sisters, Joanne and Emma, through his fatal illness and beyond. (See chapters 6, 8, 9.) Marc's family and I attend the same church and from time to time I have also been in touch with David's family.

Years have now gone by and the story still goes on. Although the two families had not met before, David's cousin Howard and Marc's sister Joanne each went to work many miles away from their separate homes. There, they met and fell in love and not long ago were married. So two special families, who had separately, through their own suffering, taught me and others so much, at last came together. Sensitised by sorrow, they now converged in celebration.

Waiting on God is creative

Trusting to the Father's love, even when tempted to think that he is not being trustworthy, may be to start on a spiritual journey which will eventually transform life, affecting other lives as well. Many people can tell how a period of personal distress led them into a closer walk with God and also gave them a deeper love for others.

To hold the pain up to the God who shares it and to trust him to redeem it, can in his time bear much fruit. The first fruit may be the encouragement it is to those who watch and wait as they witness the love, grace and even the goodness of God shining through, despite another's pain. The later fruits of such suffering, endured with his help, are often to be shared with a wider circle still.

In a radio interview about her own mentally and physically disabled son, Frances Young spoke of 'learning to be creative in circumstances which cannot be changed'. Yet the corn of wheat (or the rosehip) has to be buried before its destiny can unfold. It is usual for a time of darkness to precede the harvest.

As I finish writing this chapter, it is 25 years ago today since it was confirmed to me that I was to go to Uganda. In many ways the time spent there was wonderful but in others it was a time of great sadness and loss, nationally as well as personally. The lovely Ugandan people were brutally terrorised as the notorious Idi Amin rose to power. I had never seen so many children die as happened under my care on the wards of that teaching hospital and there were other losses, too. In retrospect, it was primarily a time to trust that whatever it looked like, God was still in final command and I had to learn to wait upon him. It was also a time to become tuned in by loss, learning to listen more carefully first to God and then to the cries of others. Looking back this was, in more ways than one, a major watershed experience in my life.

Some of the stories told in this book have come from those who have been through deeper trials, but feel they now have something precious to share. Our prayer is that in God's hands this will be used to speak to you of his loving care for all grieving children, whether small or great. Tears can act as lenses through which we learn to see and to know him better. May you find grace in your present experience, whatever it is, to hold it up to him. He can take it and shape it according to the pattern set by the life, death and rising again of our Lord Jesus Christ, as an offering to bring honour, not to you, but to him.

In his time, our loving Lord is able to use even this, perhaps your worst ever encounter with thorns, to strengthen your trust in him and to channel his energy and fruitfulness through you, and also through your children. He may take some of the best buds into his home but he still needs others here to grow to maturity and to bring his fragrance into a sick and grieving world. So may his peace gradually enfold you, quietening your thoughts and giving rest to your hearts as your hopes are fixed firmly on him to the end of your days – and beyond.

Praise be to the God and Father of our Lord Jesus Christ, the Father of compassion and the God of all comfort, who comforts us in all our troubles so that we can comfort those in any trouble with the comfort we ourselves have received from God.

(2 Corinthians 1:4)

Helpful Bible passages:
Mark 15:33–16:8
John 12:23,24
2 Corinthians 3:18
2 Corinthians 2:14–15

1 Peter 1:3–9
1 Thessalonians 4:13–18

Further reading:

Sarah Bowen, *Precious to God* (Crowborough, Christina Press 1997).

Mary Craig, *Blessings* (London, Coronet Books, Hodder and Stoughton Ltd 1979).

Alister McGrath, *Suffering* (London, Hodder and Stoughton 1992; to be reprinted).

Margaret Spufford, *Celebration* (London, Collins Fount Paperbacks 1989).

Frances Young, *Face to faith: narrative essays in the theology of suffering* (Edinburgh, T and T Clark 1990).

Helpful organisations

UK

ACT (Association for Children with Terminal and life-threatening conditions and their families), Institute of Child Health, Royal Hospital for Sick Children, St Michael's Hill, Bristol, BS2 8BJ. Tel. 01179-221556.

Cruse-Bereavement Care, 126 Sheen Road, Richmond, Surrey, TW9 1UR. Tel. 0181-940 4818 (headquarters); 0181-332 7227 (bereavement help-line). Cruse also issues a booklist to help grieving children and adults after different modes of death (sae, please).

Society of Compassionate Friends (an organisation made up of parents who have lost a child), 53 North Street, Bristol, BS3 1EN. Tel. 01179-539639.

Lone Twin Network, c/o PO Box 5653, Birmingham B29 7JY

Meditec Medical and Nursing Book Service book-list, *Children, families and death* is obtainable from:

St John's Court, Brewery Hill, Grantham, Lincs. NG31 6DW. Tel. 01476-590505.

AFRICA

East Africa: **Hospice Uganda**, PO Box 7757, Kampala, Uganda. Tel. 256 41 266867. Fax. 256 41 267488.

Southern Africa: **Society of Compassionate Friends** and **The Jewish Bereavement Association** both have branches throughout southern Africa.

ASIA

India: Developmental Paediatrics Unit, Christian Medical College and Hospital, Vellore - 632 004, India. Tel. 0416 222102.

Singapore: **Children's Cancer Foundation**, Singapore. Tel. Singapore 2970203.

AUSTRALIA

Very special kids, c/o 321 Glenferrie Road, Malvern, Victoria 3144. Tel. 03 9822 1700.

EASTERN EUROPE

St Laurence Hospice, Strada 1907, Cernavoda, Judconstanta, Romania. Tel. Cernovada 1237515 (Contact the Nurse Manager). British HQ *Children in Distress*. Tel. 01845 526272.

In addition to all of the above organisations, any major hospital dealing with dying children should have someone attached to the Paediatric Department who could advise.